Alive at the Center

ALIVE AT THE CENTER

COMTEMPORARY POEMS FROM THE PACIFIC NORTHWEST

VANCOUVER SEATTLE PORTLAND

EDITED BY

Bonnie Nish
Daniela Elza
Robin Susanto

Cody Walker
David D. Horowitz
Kathleen Flenniken

Jesse Lichtenstein
Leah Stenson
Susan Denning

PACIFIC — POETRY PROJECT

OOLIGAN PRESS

Alive at the Center
Contemporary Poems from the Pacific Northwest

ISBN13: 978-1-932010-49-7

Ooligan Press
Department of English
Portland State University
P.O. Box 751, Portland, Oregon 97207
503.725.9410 (phone); 503.725.3561 (fax)
ooligan@ooliganpress.pdx.edu
www.ooliganpress.pdx.edu

Library of Congress Cataloging-in-Publication Data is available by request.

Cover design by J. Adam Collins
Interior design by Poppy Milliken & Lorna Nakell

CONTENTS

PUBLISHER'S NOTE

Welcome to the Pacific Northwest's poetry community. You hold in your hands the inaugural publication of the Pacific Poetry Project, designed to capture this moment in poetry—the early years of the twenty-first century—from a region of North America unlike any other. We hope to bring you to the poetry salons, slams, and open-mic nights that are everywhere you look.

In the fall of 2009, a dedicated bunch of poetry lovers at Ooligan Press just happened to find themselves in the midst of a discussion about the state of poetry in our hometown—Portland, Oregon—and around the Pacific Northwest. What they came to discover was that poetry was happening all over the place in a grassroots way. Poetry represents a tiny slice of the revenue generated by the publishing industry. But as a visible and active community in our home, it is flourishing and bustling, full of life and energy. In Portland, Seattle, or Vancouver, you will find a poetry event happening weekly, if not nightly. These may be in our big bookstores, or they may be at a small wine bar, or they might even be in someone's living room, but it is a constant exchange among people who love the rhythm and meter of poetic work.

Based on this realization, Ooligan Press decided to develop an anthology of contemporary poetry from the Pacific Northwest. Very quickly, however, we realized that we were trying to do too much with one book. How could we possibly capture this buzzing, vibrant community between the covers of a single book? We couldn't. But we could launch a continuing project dedicated to two things: collecting and promoting the best poetic works from our region, and making those works available to a wider realm of readers.

Our first goal is relatively simple: we want to share the best of the best with our readers. Our second goal is a little more difficult, and slightly subversive (after all, we do live in Portland). In the last twenty or thirty years, poetry has become the provenance of a few smaller, dedicated non-profit publishers, like Copper Canyon, and of big university publishers, like the University of Pittsburgh Press (which both do amazing work). But even more, poetry seems to have become an outlier; something we used to appreciate and enjoy, but can't quite connect with now. Maybe this comes from having had to read the standard poetry fare in high school or college, which had little apparent connection to our teenage selves. Or maybe this comes from the lack of exposure and mainstream popularity of poetry, which is in part due to the fact that trade publishers don't see poetry as a financially viable product.

Whatever the cause, we think it's a shame. We think it is damaging to our cultural diversity and literary culture to be exposed to less poetry and fewer poets. Because, as Robert Duncan Gray writes in the Introduction to the book in your hands, "poetry is everywhere." So why not make poetry more "accessible"? Why not treat it like a rock star, as we do with other forms of writing? That is our goal with the Pacific Poetry Project. We want to bring poetry back to the mainstream conversation. We want to re-create the dynamic and vibrant poetry nights that happen among friends, but in the pages of these books (or on the screen of your favorite reading device). We want poetry to be for the people, as it always has been. We reject the notion that you have to "get" poetry to love it. We all get poetry. We just need to be given the permission to take whatever we do away from the reading or hearing of it. So for the publications with the Pacific Poetry Project logo on them, you are hereby given permission to think your own thoughts about the work inside. There's no right answer and there's no wrong answer. We want you to come to your own conclusions. But don't stop there. Take your thoughts and share them with a friend. Make poetry part of your conversation. Quote it on your favorite social network. Give it to your friends and family.

We are on a mission to bring poetry to the people. We need your help to do it. Enjoy *Alive at the Center* and welcome to the Pacific Poetry Project.

—Ooligan Press

ALIVE AT THE CENTER

(AN INTRODUCTION)

Everything is super. Super duper.

Imagine Poetry (with a capital P) as a functional member of society. Poetry gets a day job and earns a sizable paycheck. Poetry purchases two luxury Mercedes Benzes and gives one to me—a brand new, shiny Mercedes Benz! Super duper. The inside smells like lavender honey. I bake Poetry a chocolate cake, by which I mean to say, Thank You. It doesn't turn out perfect, but Poetry doesn't seem to care—so nonchalant!—Poetry eats three big slices of my imperfect chocolate cake. Oh, all that chocolate all over Poetry's face!

Fantastic.

Lately I have been thinking about poetry with a lowercase p, so naturally I am worried. I have also been thinking about death, salt, and hot water—or more specifically, deathsalt and hotwater. I have written a mathematical equation:

$p = 4(hw) + (ds)$

Where p = poetry, h = hot, w = water, d = death and s = salt.

I have also written an accompanying recipe:

Poetry à la mode

> Combine four parts hotwater with one part deathsalt in a clean glass bowl.
>
> Stir vigorously with soft hands.
>
> Serve with ice cream.

A beekeeper friend of mine has a swarm up for grabs. I am worried about the poetry of it. I guess I am worried about the poetry fading or weakening in certain spots. What would we do for a poem compared to what we would do for, say, a taco? And is there really all that much difference between a poem and a taco?

If all the poets of the world die, what then of poetry? What if all the good poets died? Would good poetry be dead? Is poetry dependent on poets? I don't think so, but really I don't know.

I believe that poetry is not necessarily site-specific. You can find a poem anywhere. You can find ten poems in bed, an entire volume inside your kitchen—you certainly don't need to leave the house to write. There is plenty of poetry all around. Poetry tucked in the sock drawer and under the couch. Poetry amongst the sharp knives. In the bathtub—hotwater. Deathsalt in the potatoes. Nothing is safe. That being said, go outside. It's nice outside.

I find a lot of poems at work, which is a bummer because I am at work. I find poems whilst riding my bicycle, which is also a bummer because I am riding my bicycle. It is often inconvenient to write a poem. Some poems must be ignored, or rather left alone—"ignored" seems harsh. Some poems remain free and that's super. Some poems are lost and some are eternally found. Whatever. Super duper. No big deal.

Sometimes I find poems perfect and easy. Poetry can be so easy. That's a big secret. Poets don't generally like to talk about it; perhaps we worry that such a declaration might lessen the value of our work. Truth be told, sometimes poetry is piss-easy and most of the time it carries no inherent value whatsoever. I come home from work and take all my clothes off in the kitchen. I say hello to the cat. I walk through the house to the bedroom and lie down. I get high and lost in the blades of the ceiling fan. I go to the bathroom and stare at myself in the mirror for a short while. Then I return to the bedroom, lie on the bed and the rest of the evening is all about poetry. I walk naked from room to room and find poems waiting for me. Eager poems rolling around. Belly-up poems. I hardly write, yet at the end of the night I have accumulated twenty poems or more! It must be some kind of magic.

Poetry is everywhere.

I once watched Ed Skoog recite poems in the middle of the night in an underground parking lot. I once watched Emily Kendal Frey recite poems on the third floor of a shopping mall. It happens in the weirdest places, under the most unlikely circumstances. Poetry seems to be all around, occupying the spaces in which we least expect to find it.

So here we are.

You hold in your hands a flock of poems. A gathering, yes. An organized pastiche poured fresh from the top left corner of America. American poetry is alive and well. American poetry is healthy. There is so damn much of it! How does this happen? A great many people share this huge experience, some sort of life in America, and feel the urge to report back. There are things here we feel must be shared, passed on. It is a beautiful thing. Super.

Upon reading this collection, one cannot help but feel a great sense of relief. Everything is super. Poetry is fat and fun and full of beauty. Super duper. The problems we face today are bigger and more complicated than those we faced yesterday, but rest assured—there is poetry in between, around and inside everything, and every day we are getting better and better at exposing it. Everything is going to be just fine.

I have written a recipe for this book.

Alive at the Center

Combine four parts hotwater, one part deathsalt, a dash of fresh ginger, a clove of crushed garlic, five pickled pigs feet, one sea anemone, three tusks, two bundles of cashmere, a pint of Puget Sound, a rumble of kitten purr, a chorus of traffic jam, two pocketfuls of lavender honey, a whalebone of satisfied hunger and two feet of sadness, a lungfull of unmelodious childsong, a mile of rusted train track, a never ending ambulance siren, two slices of cold cheese pizza, raw beef on the edge, fresh hoof, warm blood of beet, nine bridges, a dash of Douglas Fir, a waterfall of black coffee and one day-old donut. Salt and pepper to taste. Stir vigorously with soft hands. Serve with ice cream and imperfect chocolate cake.

Everything is super.

—Robert Duncan Gray

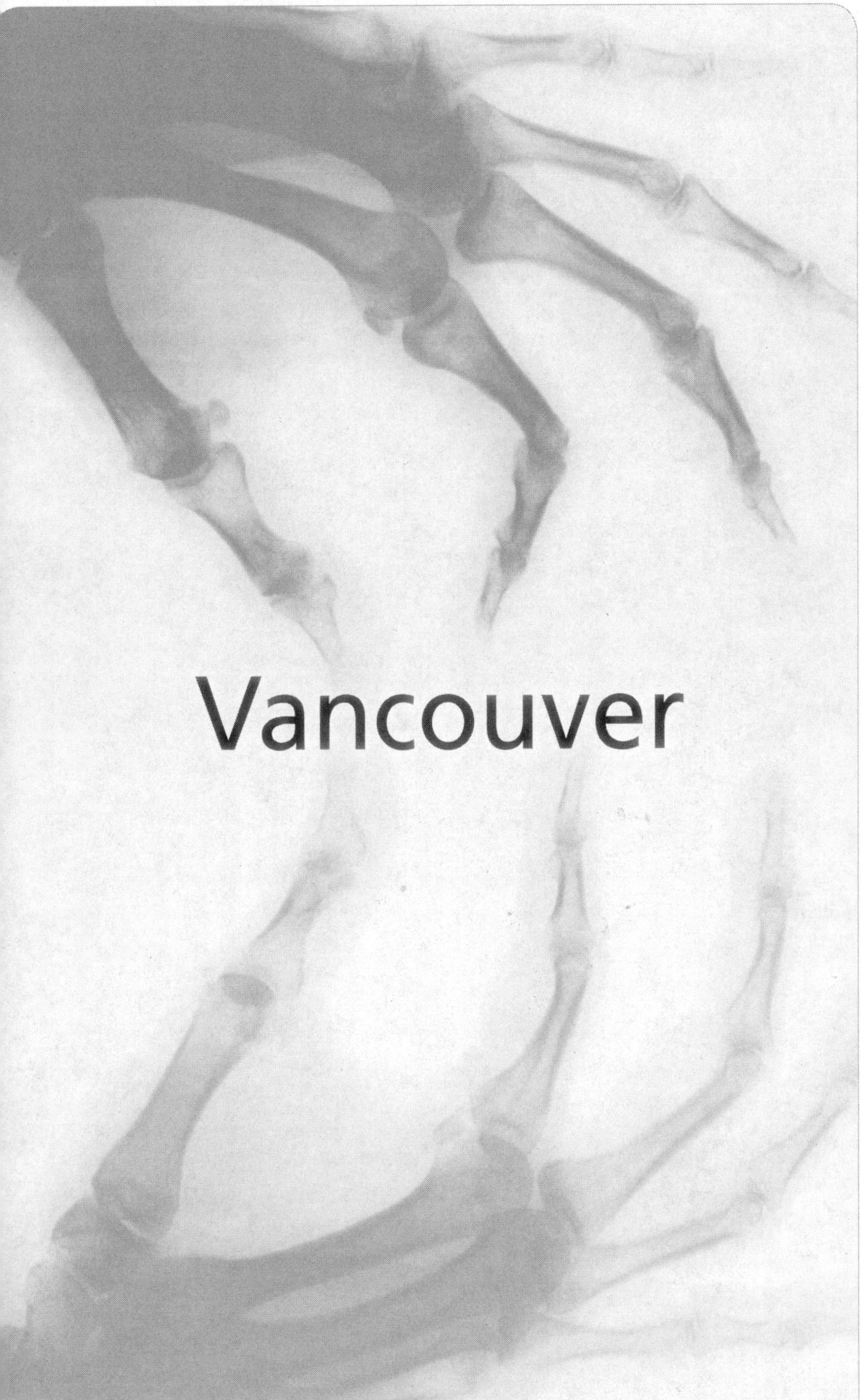

Vancouver

POEMS FROM VANCOUVER, BRITISH COLUMBIA

One thing has been clear from the start: to attempt to represent the poetry voices in Vancouver—present and future—is a bold undertaking, if not an impossible one. We will not be presumptuous about the future or claim that we have entirely covered the present. What we can claim is to have presented a mere taste of Vancouver's richness in poetry.

One vital aspect of an anthology for me is the possibility for a gathering—the opportunity to create a community. As editors, we wanted to offer a selection that crossed over, through, and into different poetic sensibilities by way of established poets, new poets, work published and unpublished, and a diversity of themes.

I want to extend my sincere gratitude to Bonnie Nish and Robin Susanto for accompanying me through the challenges and joys of this adventure.

The three of us invited 125 poets to mark Vancouver's 125th anniversary. We focused on poets whose voices we had heard in libraries, cafés, on the streets, in reading series, at festivals… These included poets who work hard at organizing and supporting spaces in which poetry can be heard. We asked around for recommendations, for representatives of different communities, for names we could not afford to miss. We were interested in including people who represent different schools, trends, and blends. In the meantime, I was reading poetry book after poetry book and requesting poems.

Midway through, there was a postal strike, which added an unexpected twist to the process. We requested both electronic and paper submissions to make sure that at least one of them reached us. (Our sincere apologies if some work never made it.)

If I had to sum up the approach, I would call it *poetic*. We put some constraints in place and stayed open to what showed up. We appreciated convergence and serendipity. All three editors had to agree on the poems selected. We were pleased to discover the overlap between us, and where there wasn't agreement we had to pull out the "convince me" card. We made very few compromises and tried to keep politics out of this harvest. One thing is for sure: most of the poems we've brought to you have been spoken into the Vancouver air and know its seasons.

We debated at length if we, the editors, should submit poems. We decided against it, but then I began to feel that it would be unfair not to show up for the gathering. And if I was going to show up, then I did not want the other two editors excluded. It boiled down to an "all or nothing" decision. We were in this together, along with Vancouver's poets.

We hope the value here is not simply in offering you a sampling of poets' work, but in offering a chance to become more acquainted, more related, to a bigger community. This anthology gives us the added benefit of expanding this community across three cities. Mix, mingle, enjoy.

Kind Regards

—Daniela Elza

A CURSED POEM

I

If you leave me
I'll put a curse on you:

I'll embed my eyes,
under your ribs
to wake you at night
and look through you;

I'll glue my skin
on your fingertips
not to touch a thing
without feeling me.

I'll nail my scent into every
Spring petal,
when you smell a flower,
my scent to stab you.

II

If I leave you,
because of a look
because of a word or two,
because of a subtle quiver
because of the time
that drips down the window,
because of the tender rapture.

Blind, I will walk on Earth;
It will rain endlessly,
I will drown unaware.

A LIGHTNESS DANCES

a lightness dances
a tangle of wet hair gathers
momentum; she cries
look mama, here's my cartwheel!
her limbs blur
whir in a gymnastic mist
and with a soft thump
resolve against the grass

splayed on the ground she laughs
and sighs, a snowless angel
my heavenless angel
I laugh and cry to see her
at night when she curls
suddenly long arms and legs
in futile fetal pose

because she's already born
we're all squeezed into daylight
against our will
together we squint at the sun
take baby steps
hold hands

she holds out her arms
begs I take her back in time
the sun keeps rising
suspended like a pendulum
counting our hours down

AFTER THE TSUNAMI

The sea is all wrong
Its surging sullen, its shimmer thick as pitch
Its waves stammer as they crash
Headfirst with the crack of bones
Whole coasts swept with splinters of syllables
Whole islands told without a tongue

The wind spoke, instead of breeze
The hundred thousand names that no longer belong
Names that are called, names that don't answer

But still you touch your lips to the sea
Run your hand over the water, as if it was the fur of a sleeping animal
To whisper to the sea the houses and the vegetable gardens
The fisher folks, and the tourists who came to sleep softly on the sand
The little children who held on briefly before closing their eyes
The hundred thousand names,
Names that are whispered, names that are released

(And I have seen the whole world whispering with you
Lining whole continents with lit candles
Emptying its pockets into the sea)

Now you who belong to the sea must lull the sea to sleep
Lull the sea to sleep

ALLEY FRAGMENT AND NAME

Pull a fortune from the alley; card of wisdom reversed or blessed

Corrugated cardboard alley (say painted red)

A river of alley: where window of light, window shades drawn
Slick spill of pollen and milk
And this is neighborhood drawn by alley

Someone wrote a message, rolled it, slid it inside a bottle, sealed it, tossed it into the
alley…

So winds and current might lift it away.

Shadow alley—wild electric sizzle—touch with the eye alley

Peel back the walls of the house; exposed beam, night sky, negative space
Touch alley of bolt and screw; touch steel, acrylic, orange

Dance in the alley, why not? Head touch the ground. Broken alley pours out light.

Here in the narrow of grate and pail; corner of copper patched over

Pipe of echo; aluminum; hollow to sky alley; darker pallet of rain
(Do you remember where you placed this dab of yellow?)
Spackle alley, rubbed smooth, made rough. Pull fingers free from gloves, touch

Uncork the message, run nail along wax, waft of whisky and whimsy, crack

Perhaps it is a love letter to alley. Perhaps answer to our prayer.

What is endless

This room is alley. So is your heart

APPLETON

Hookah squats on carpet, Buddha-
esque. Undulating spirals of sapphire
smoke hula up her nose. That buzz.
That buzz that slows your blood,

calls you back to bed like a lover.
Soothes your inner asshole.
BC bud. Best bud
in the world. Worth risking jail for.

High-resolution satellite images.
Narcs' warrant executed Tuesday.
Grow-op raided Wednesday.
Dozens of firearms. Five thousand plants.

Big bust for a small town, says Constable Cook.
For export, for sure. Cultivation facilities dismantled.
Straight people relieved. Green party over,
but Zoe cried. It was the best job ever!

Dope dealers pay well. Her boyfriend
sold product at school. Their responsibilities
included digging a tunnel under the border,
blaming black fingernails and muddy jeans
on dirt biking at the gravel pit.

Parents were shocked. We thought she was
on Facebook, chatting. We thought he was
on the Internet, with her, boy's father chiding,
it's APPLE ton, son, not Marijuanaton!

AT WOOD-EDGE ROAD

The city seems too green
to be inhabited by death.

One expects blood immediately
to grow into the trunk and branches of red
alder, to find the nova of its spiral galaxy,
its clotted pods of crushed crimson, exploded
in the victim's head, laid daintily,
face-down on the asphalt. A posy of mini
daffodils under a tree, nearby—this troop of yellow-haired
girl guides, set to lead across the black lea
of the road, stops, in order not to disturb
the least detail in the yellow-jacketed,
taped and labelled crime scene—curbed,
their own glorious colour, perplexed
by the awful similarity.

ATTEMPTS TO KNOW THE PAST

I do not want to say *darkness* or *door*,
or *the dark door we walk in through.*
This is no way to understand the past.
Will write instead of those regions on maps
coloured in by the imagination. Or the dusk
that is the backdrop of the universe—
how, when I was a child, I pictured space
hanging like a painting on a huge white canvas
inside a gilded frame. Infinity a notion that could
send a person over the edge, as in those Sinbad films
where whole ships careen over earth's steep curb,
and men gallop past the known periphery,
flogging their animals into the sea.

I will not write of the absence of light,
God's holy show, ripe orchards tilting their fruit
to the heavens. Or of the sun tossed like a gold coin
into the bucket of the sky. Instead I'll praise
what I have before me: a book, a lamp,
a chair beside the open window, a pocket watch
whose hour is caught in the glass eye of the moon.
The thread of history as dun-coloured
as a corridor in a painting by Vermeer.
Knock once on a Street in Delft, watch a woman
asleep at her table, look through the slant
entrance to the room beyond. All these portals.
Apertures that could take us anywhere.

The womb a door. The past a door. There,
I've said it. The future a bright yellow bird
in the corner of the room, singing. How easily
we fall off the map, sail into new worlds distracted
by song. Once, I stood in the National Museum lost
for hours in the radiant sheenof a pearl earring.
Terrible monsters here, they said, of those realms
where anything could happen, where anything

did happen. Who was I yesterday? The day before?
How have the rooms of the past remembered me,
if they remember me at all? Open a door onto the pitch
of space, onto the sunless caves we came from.
What sadness there, what hope, what delirium.

AUNT JENNY

A fallen bridge
in your eyes,
and on the far side
the lilies of lucidity.

Satan called you out
into the garments of death—
convinced you
to swallow those pills.

And you lay dying
in your room for two days,
slipping into dreams,
as cool green water
trickled over your skin;

you were prom queen,
a princess of sunflowers
in your youth.

But then you were Ophelia.

That awkward word,
the diagnosis
stretches between us like green rope, or
a fallen bridge.
And on the far side—
lilies. And I cry
for the broken stem
of your mind.

BEACHES

She and I talk about home like it's the first pair of underwear you picked out for yourself. Didn't pinch; developed holes; etc. Home is the first place you live without your parents, we decide, because we are like that.

Her boyfriend is mop-headed, grins like a kid with a bucket and spade. Sometimes she's the beach and sometimes she's the mom, saying Sunscreen, fer chrissakes, sunscreen. I prefer to say partner, have also heard sweetheart. I dunno, yet, if I have a partner or a sweetheart or what. You've stuck your legs out one side of the umbrella, she says, and stayed mostly in the shade. She cracks a joke about fish aplenty.

What we are going to do with our lives: work with our hands? The way people who think about home as underwear work with their hands. The way they always go home. And what of our loves? Well, we'll write poetry the way fishmongers write poetry, knifing a steelhead open like a cherished book.

BEER, BLOOD & BUKOWSKI

We didn't quite know it at the time
but we were making art—
the night we got kicked out of three bars
chasing ghosts across Vancouver.

You were heartbroken, drunk on whisky
I was heartbroken, intoxicated by anger.

We raised fists to the shadow of a smug moon
before downing a pint toasting our misfortune.

No one wants a lonely drunk, you shouted
somewhere between Water & Carrel Street.

You had your nose broken
when you hit on the tattooed bartender
busted your lip wide open

when you started rambling
something about the masquerade of the Haida Indian
and the desperation in Bukowski's poetry.

I fell off my bar stool laughing
when you mixed up the two images.

That night, stumbling back to East Van
dripping with beer and blood
we were a walking Pollock painting
giggling all the way home
wondering why no one was offended
over Bukowski.

BORDER BOOGIE (1969)

You who go out on schedule
to kill, do you know
there are eyes that watch you?
—Denise Levertov

1
Moon-pent in a white vw,
heading up the freeway north from Seattle,
sperm-like rain snaking up the windshield
toward Nirvana, British Columbia,

I am twenty-two
and deathless.

My boyfriend Tim and I slip
across the border just after Blaine
where he blew his mind on acid
a month ago on our first reconnaissance
of the route, hip, cool, tuned
to Coltrane's A Love Supreme.

2
The horrors of Hanoi,
napalm stuck in our skulls,
Levertov's logged words
encoding my journal.

Simon Fraser's radical curriculum
promises manna for the disenchanted,
tales of students storming the faculty lounge,
"Be in's" for beleaguered flowering ones.

Tim drags along, averse to academics,
burying his letter from the draft board
deep in his duffle bag, moving
breathless past customs officials.

3
His dad chose for him a military career.
He told me how in officers' training
he leapt from a helicopter,
shot and skinned a rabbit, vomited,
then heaved himself out of there,

"tuned in, turned on, dropped out,"
found Monty his guru, and
a macrobiotic regime till I
caught him munching an O Henry.

Returning from a seminar on Blake
and the mythopoetic mind, I
became "The Little Girl Lost"
who found her lion deep

into Cream and Miles,
sprawled on the orange shag rug,
headphones riveted to his ears,
an astronaut trolling inner space,

splayed like Da Vinci's man,
skinny, open-faced.

4
He graduated (barely) in physics
but sought the Tao of imagination,

did piecework, house painting,
lineman jobs, stoned, toked up,

and with his first cheque bought me
a shimmering shift of red-orange glitter,
Aphrodite dress from a head shop.

He followed me to Vancouver,
pining for home, yet home meant

the draft and Vietnam,
hot killing fields and hollowed eyes.

5
Up all night typing papers on Poe's Berenice,
and Ligeia, I take to sporting dark capes,
grow pale with anemia,
believe that in another incarnation
I had been Poe's child wife Virginia Clemm.
(I always become what I research.)

My thesis grows pregnant with itself,
swells to 300 pages, mysterious,
white, like Moby Dick.

Tim, restless, disenchanted,
drives back and forth to Seattle.
We who had considered marriage,

split. I touch his head one last time
and choose to stay in Canada:
first hostel, hotel,
and finally, home.

6
Stuck with unknowing
all these years, I wonder:

Did he get snared by the draft?
Did he break and bleed in Southeast Asia?
Is his name inscribed on the wall in Washington?

Or is he a banker now,
easing into late mid-life
with a wife, a dog, and grandchildren on the way?

Googling gives no leads.
But who really needs to know?
The slide of sex, the glimmer gone,

all seems impossible, improbable
to my 60-something life.

Nevertheless, I would offer
more than ironies:
this last image of him falling
downstairs in a pool of his own light.

Errant knight,
held in a poem's peace.

CABIN FEVER

If I had a bottle of wine up here, I'd hold the neck in my fist and tip it up too fast. Let the weight of it rip through the long dusty day right to my feet. Like rain. Or a road. Or somewhere to go.

If I had a bottle of wine, I'd lie on the ground and practise at happy drunk. Despite a hundred feet of good ladder and the thrill of distance in the dark. Or that place under the hatch where the ladder cage opens to the sky and you lean back, harnessless, into it. Because you can't climb with a bottle in your hand, I'd say. Knowing a thousand famous men have proven me wrong.

Or I'd sit here and love this place like they would. All the good trees. Fireweed tender as a second chance, not knowing what came before. The things men tell each other when they're drunk. How conversation, even love, becomes a ladder, and they climb anything that goes up.

Hammock, I'd think. Sky. Runaway sun. I could eat corn and run open-mouthed and greasy into the woods where the sun went. Maybe it's simple as a picnic table with a pot of boiling corn. Easy as forgetting my fear of the strangers who roll up my driveway at dusk. Waving them closer with butter on my hands, grease stains on my pants where I wipe off my palms. Corn, I'd say, kernels filling my mouth. A mouth full of perfect days. The butter ground down to the bottom of its thin metal wrapper. The endless shucking of corn.

I could love this place right. Serve up summer night like fall-apart homemade dessert. But before I do, I find Al Purdy's already chewed it up and spat it out perfect, and I hate him for it. Running and running naked with summer in your mouth. Fuck you, Al Purdy. I run my teeth over the kernels of all my favourites. Wanting to see them suffer. But no. They do that already. So beautifully.

It seems they are always drinking. Or undoing the drinking of their past. The hard glamour of damage. Polished like infidelity, like leaving. Why try? I think. When they've already been here so much better and drunker and more foolish with love.

I turn to offer them more corn, but they're gone. Have thrown their husks on the grass and called it beautiful. Even laughter is a ladder. Have left their garbage and taken my truck. Are drinking my wine a bottle each like beer. Are looking for another roadside stand. Hey, I yell, but it's twenty cents a cob and six for a buck. It's summer. It's corn. It's so fucking cheap. They hold a twenty out the window and watch it flap. Six for a dollar. One good hot night. Somewhere to go. Corn. Corn so sweet you eat it raw. Windows cranked. Gasoline. That perfect speed that comes with its own warm wind.

CARS

cars drift down
sw Marine Drive

a long prose sentence
on Valium

the beginning forgets
all syntactical energies

the amnesiac sentence
refuses the period's finality

in this senseless sentence
with no beginning or end

some cars pull while others push
no train of linear thought

a sentence can be stepped
into only once, never again

lines on a map, lines in a story
a long breath that might last

CELL PHONE

Once only important people like pilots
or battery commanders needed to know
everything as it happened, but now, like a medical intern
I too am on call twenty-fours a day
with no data too trivial not to warrant an interruption:
at the opera its urgent beep disturbs
Pavarotti's "Nessun Dorma" How could anyone sleep?
Its trill protests halfway through
the memorial service at the cenotaph.
Like a concealed weapon or a portable Buddha,
it goes with me everywhere, stakes a claim on me,
when I am "eating or opening a window or just walking dully along."
And when I answer I am always aware
of being overheard. Privacy? I *want* even strangers to know
the important deals I make, the assignations.
And anyway this amulet protects me
against surprises, like now that ten-ton truck
that abruptly appears from the right in mid-sentence
while I'm travelling at eighty through a red light
and frames my last…

CROWS

'Cras' (Latin) means 'tomorrow.'

Out of all four corners of the world,
these ancients with tomorrow on their tongues
gather one by one,

cackle from whatever throne
they find to occupy—
at the edges of our eyes, the crows'

feet etch our every smile,
as if the only thing in life that matters
is our laughter.

Creatures of both earth and sky, they do not
care if we believe them evil,
dread them as death's messengers

or simply scorn them for the mess they make
scavenging through garbage in the park.
Always dressed for funerals,

crows know they are the pallbearers for our souls,
their gift, to find the glitter in what we leave behind.

DESDEMONA (DURGA)

he came at me in a fierce rage
i felt a small crack open in my
forehead, Kali
burst forth and struck him
a fierce blow
and he was felled
Kali continued
moving about the scene
devouring men high and low
and then
i said, *stop*
not the shaper
her eyes strayed toward Emilia
and again
i said, *stop*
with the place now cleared
but for the four left standing
Kali returned to slip inside
my head
i went to the cupboard
for rags and salt
i opened the closet
for the mop and bucket
started running cold water

no idea what Iago or Emilia
will do with themselves, but
a woman needs to keep her
attention on what she herself
needs to do: every good bloodbath
must be followed by a scrub and rinse,
a home is not a battlefield after all

EVERYDAY THINGS

If everything is sacred
you will use the knife carefully.

The meal you will place on the table
will nourish more than the body.

The vow you take to serve
will turn sacrifice to pleasure.

If all things carry meaning
you will let pain heal.

No matter if your home is one room
you will place a flower to greet the light.

If blessings often come disguised, you
will take home the thin dog with the sad eyes.

FORGETTING MR. LOW

Downtown on the Eastside
where diners close late
with metal bars
strapped up against the flat belly of a doorway,
rumours spread faster than rolling paper
between junkies and pushers.
It's Saturday morning, early, three am.
Vans begin to roam the streets
looking for good drugs, bad girls
and Mr. Low sits in his corner, undisturbed
as a buzz begins to stir in an already buzzing street life.
Pimps scream up and down the road
ready to jump on encroaching vendors
while their girls smoke cigarettes in bunches,
hunched under a street light
with skirts hiked up almost to their pelvic bones,
night air slips under to remind them business is slow,
the long fingers of hunger
stretch across their thinning young bodies
pushed to the limit of uncaring.

Mr. Low shifts position
lifts his eyes down the street
where a tomb has formed in the alleyway.
Boys pounding boys into the pavement
screams in the night,
the sound of an empty bed,
a mother's terror,
wakes her miles away.
Mr. Low listens,
shuts his eyes and remembers,
there were times when women touched him,
boys followed him,
now he sits as drool drips down his double chin
into his soaking lap.
A siren startles him, someone pokes him.
"Hey old man! Go home."
Mr. Low nods, they move on.
He waits for the smell of coffee

from across the street to permeate the air,
until then he sits comfortably watching, undisturbed.

The buzz is quietening to a dim hustle
the hookers have all been picked up,
their pimps sleep on cots
in the cramped boarded rooms
of a burnt out building.
The boys have bandaged their cuts
and gone home to mother
while the morning dew settles
on Mr. Low's shoes
and he knows he is forgotten,
just as he forgets.

GHOSTAL OR VANCOUVER'S GEOGRAPHY OF LOSS

Beyond the Ovaltine, before Save On Meats, O, I have closed myself
to this, the shopping carts heavy with cardboard, rigs, clothing, bicycle parts,
people alien because, I know this now too much, drugs have abducted them until
there is only, what I saw you become, a hunger and I have stopped wanting
to give. As I pass fast and blind through the homeless, their transactions with
dealers a dance, a man, not you but still it could have been, careens towards me,
overcoat, hoodie, arms extended in leftover desire,
"Honey, where you been all my life, you're so beautiful," he says, knowing
I will ignore him, what else can I do, stirred by how long it takes to kill
longing, and yet, not wanting to be touched, ever again, your ghost down here,
might have been you, how can I forgive this, grey day, boarded-up buildings,
you dead and I no longer able to feel for the lost of the earth, wanting to breathe
immune for a while in the pure and shining lie of you not gone, us with plans,
the man with outstretched arms clean, embraced by loved ones, not passed
by cold on the pavement between Save On Meats, the Ovaltine.

HANG ON

The bus driver says
"hang on,"
and I want to say,
sir, I am hanging on
as best I can:
to the post,
to my head,
to my partner,
to the Earth.
But my life is falling through
my fingers
like fine white sand,
and this grasping—
well, we all know
the thing we grasp at
eludes us
all the more.
You implore us to
hang on, and sir, I
know you mean well,
but I think in all fairness
we require more
explicit instruction.

"Hang on to
the thought that birthed us,
to the fullness of our hearts,
to the present love that
fuels each moment.
Hang on to the Light,
to the wisdom of the ages,
to the spirit that rushes
through your pen,
to the calm beneath the pain,
to the fast-flowing river
that underlies all sorrow.
Hang on to your faith in
the ever-changingness of everything,
in goodness,

and white, wild-growing freesia."
And you, too, sir,
you must hang on
for all of us:
to your belief in
the power of the road
to deliver us to
our destinies;
to your commitment to this route and
the work of ferrying your
fellow-travelers
from place to place.
Perhaps the key is
for all of us to hang on,
but loosely.
Maybe with an
open stance and
relaxed arms we can better
flow with the bumps and
sudden stops along
this winding roadway.
And it does wind, sir,
and even you,
who drive it every day,
must be jarred
from time to time
by the unpredictable actions of
people and machines.

Sir, my stop has come,
and I bid you a
good evening,
wishing only that
you may grip
loosely to the
road, which bends and
sways like a tree limb
in the breeze,
but tightly to
hope,
for yourself and
for us all,

your passengers on this
sacred vessel,
this ambling
gliding
careening
living
dream.

HOLLOW

Suddenly I am hollowed out, at the lip
of weeping, panic in my throat, because
        the season changes, and into the pause
        between the shifting moments slips
a blankness unprepared for, and someone's
leaving, and all my plans come undone.

Nor does it help that the dark
falls early, the clouds blocking light
        so even a pleasant walk cannot ignite
        inside me the necessary spark
of hopefulness that gives a shape to each hour
that fights off what comes to devour

the little I've now become: alone
to make the day, routine not yet kicked in.
        I kick the sidewalk trash while within
        whirls my own lean cyclone
sucking from me what once I was: one whose joy
at living and arriving was not so easy to destroy.

HUMMINGBIRDS

Jacked up on sugar, they zip-line
over teens in jean cutoffs
whose hands brush, interlock.

As they scout the park's perimeter
for a secluded nook, territorial males show off,
ascend thirty feet in a surge of hormones

only to free fall: a rufous blur.
Whirligigs in a gale wind, hearts
displayed in their bright throats.

Spring stoppered in a bird
no bigger than your thumb—
the urge to screw around

in the back of a car, forget
who you are, put beak to
stamen, drink it all.

IN EVENT OF MOON DISASTER

In the summer of 1969, William Safire wrote the address Nixon would give the nation if Neil Armstrong and Edwin Aldrin became stranded on the lunar surface with no hope of rescue. It was entitled "In Event Of Moon Disaster."

In event of moon disaster,
do not think
that we have put men
in robot bodies without reason

That perhaps the eleven layer A7L spacesuit
is padded casket comfortable
Instead,
remember that those careful white costumes
are the smallest Eden
we have ever put an Adam inside of

Do not think of weightless suffocation

Think instead of your children
with their heads under their desks
of the smell of coffee
burning your re-entry into the kitchen
the initials pocket knifed into the bus window
the footprints in steady dust

Do not feel weighted by the lead clothes you wear
in case the bomb drops.
            They are not as heavy as you think

JOY

I was at a house party celebrating Canada Day
when I met a woman named Joy.
I said: "It's a joy to meet you Joy."
She beamed at me,
then said: "I am manic depressive."
At once the conversation dried up.
Not knowing what to say
made an excuse
I had to call my girlfriend.
A lie.
I avoided her staying upstairs
while she waited lost in the party below.
She reminded me of a dog I once had.
Aalways happy to see me,
jumping and licking my face,
overwhelmed by its affection,
I fled upstairs, afraid to come down.
Eventually my mother lost her patience:
"OK, we'll give him away to the S.P.C.A."
She made me accompany her.
I carried the dog in my arms.
It looked at me with the saddest eyes,
wavering on the brink of tears.
He spoke to me:
"Don't leave me."
I swear I did not imagine it.
By the time we arrived at the S.P.C.A.,
I said: "Mum I change my mind
I want to keep him."
"No. After all the trouble
you've caused me,
dragging me all the way here,
you don't deserve a dog."

I am sorry Joy.
I was afraid.
I didn't understand
until I too was diagnosed manic-depressive
eight years ago on Valentine's Day of all days.
This is the way I feel every time
I am led back to the psych ward,
an obedient dog
crying to God, don't leave me.

MANNING PARK IN THE DARK

The night we came through the storm
and survived, I loved my life for the first time.
The world was white, there were no other cars
on the winding highway to light our way
as we climbed the summit of the mountain pass,
anchored by instinct to the vanishing road.
We were alone on our approach
to Summerland, roped to life
by a single strand of breath—
I breathed in and out
as we sped around curve after curve
in the blindness, the road gone under our feet
but for the slick of tires sticking to snow,
the guiding lines invisible,
white paint under white flurry.
The screen of the windshield blazed
our sight with filaments of bright,
snow whipping horizontal towards us
like a million stars from the universe.
Then I was calm. I let go.
I could have fallen forward forever,
the air tasting like honey,
stillness opening at the centre of my body,
I wanted it to go on forever.
Breath, silence, piano music
faintly stirring from the CD player,
strings guiding us down into a valley
pillowed in fog, lights twinkling
in the small towns. Then the arc of a flashlight
through the air, the animal
lying across the road in a heap
of flesh as if asleep,
the screeching swerve back into our lives.

MEH'S ON CBC!

whod'a thought this worn paper immigrant
would be on canada's national radio its voice and thought

(used to think CBC was what made you canadian
'cause authentic canadians seemed to be always saying
'did you hear the CBC yesterday' 'last nite on CBC'
but there was something wrong with us 'cause we'd rather listen
    to 50's doo-wop and motown on the goldie oldies station
    I admit there was a time I tried to listen but my ears would
        slip lips and so would time mime a part-time canadian
        no I'm not connected to the country no ear to the ground-
-ing nation the catsup chip state of mainly unity)

meh is so proud at last she's being noticed
'so the secrets of your shan cooking is out'
people'd said words dashed with her own exclamations
secrets are watched out!

during the interview she puts on her best english
handles it like pro unlike the minced languages she normally uses
chopping thai shan and english other accents picked up second-hand
she explains things as I'd never heard her explain to me
and though I turn away from the microphone I can't help staying to overhear

(later she asks me, 'did you hear my story?'
as if telling the reporter was a way of telling me
and I admit the stuff I hear is stuff for keeps)

every once in a while standing before the stove
stirring chicken curry and frying slices of golden *topu*
she can't help it, her hand automatically reaches up flicks on the exhaust fan
even though the noise is overwhelming and annoys the reporter
she's worried about the house stinking up smell a sensitive thing
but for the most part she concedes to the reporter and turns it off

'tell me' says the reporter, 'what do you think about when you smell these
    foods?'
and meh who's never been asked that kind of question
but who likes to humor the game anyway
answers
'that I'm hungry.'

MOUNT PLEASANT

under the weather or above the fault lines, there has been no measurable change in our mental health. we brace for "the big one," whatever that means. blush of pink blooms against the landscape. we could chart our progress against tectonic plates and topographical maps but common sense would dictate we limit such questionable use of our already limited resources. which is to say, hand me an upper. what small philosophical forces are gathering momentum behind the counters of this city's bakeries and in languages unfamiliar to our ears? we have grown fat in recent months and unprepared for evacuation. pink buds on branches and blouses. we engage in commerce and call it action. which is to say, i bought a sweater and ate a cookie. alone and isolated in the basement suites of the lower east side, we ponder our day jobs and indulge ourselves in the existential crises du jour. imagine to reach some lofty heights, as if we were on the second floor, as if we were Baudelaire. surely Foucault never drank so much coffee in one sitting, and Virginia Woolf wrote in spite of, and not because of, her depression. you might argue that one good Stein deserves another but i am tired and i have been kicked out of every cafe on Main Street for crimes against the artist-run collective. no, you can't use the bathroom, i just washed the floor. this hourglass is impatient and catches up with us. we are too easily distracted by the fashions of the time. when we return to the car it is covered with cherry blossoms. an innocuous landscape amidst the rush of cars. is that a hooker? such detritus, this daily existence. a little room, a beast to scratch, and a warm body to lean up against. how can we measure our progress against the inimitable forces of consumerism in the distance? we haven't shaved in weeks. and guilt, that useless emotion, chafes. somewhere a raccoon clambers up a wire fence with an evil glint in his eye. still the blossoms fall and we use them to wipe the tears off each other's faces.

NADINE

Night of quick, wild rain, gusts off the inlet. Blackness
lit only by glintings of rain, bored through to nothing
by my car headlights. I stood waiting on the pier.
She stepped out of the blackness and into dim sheen
and faced me, saying nothing yet gesturing. At first,
I thought that she didn't speak English. Then her friend
was there beside her, down from an unseeable ship.
The three of us piled into my taxi. I apologized
for not realizing that she couldn't speak or hear.
The two of them in the back seat, the friend giggled,
chattered half to himself, while she sat forward, leaned
to the side and looked out at me from where
she was never to be woven into the sound of a voice
and where she seemed hidden, even when she displayed
her widest smile, her hand on my shoulder, touching at me
to turn, turn left, turn, turn right—knowing I knew the way,
and at every instant teasing, flirting. Then the laughter
in her eye-flash in the rearview mirror undid me,
the clamped-down face with which I peddled myself
trip by trip fell away. We were together, the three of us,
the wind at the black glass around us the breath
of a childlike presence welcoming us further, further,
the rain on the roof the tapping of a heart. They taught me
how to sign *no problem, friend and asshole.*
They were Similkameen, they were my age,
and had been in Vancouver a month. They had gotten
an American twenty-dollar bill for the taxi fare
from the ship to their hotel and back again. They gave me
all of it, refusing the change, the money adding up
to more than a decent tip. The friend, the girl's cousin,
her sarcastic, playful, hilarious pimp, told me
the sailors had made fun of her, and neither of them
stood for that. Anyhow, the sailors sent her back. *Get us somebody else,*
they said. *We want a talking whore.*

OFFERING

faith hides in little pockets like the heart
& the throat. born with a serious streak
the width of an altar, i climb the stairs in
that first home, the zhi ma wu, black
sesame childhood sweet, squeeze soya
beans in a rough white cotton bag, hold
my mother's workworn hands. what do
any of these small gestures mean
except that they have carried me
into now? shadows in the corner.
dust on the shelves & in the blood. an
archival endeavour, let the fragments
stand together, make us larger than the
sum of the individuals. float from
quote to quote, to shore the body of
a man with hairy legs, a mi'kmaq
woman with dark hair who curls into
the sheets like a child, a gay boy who
made the best damn bannock i've ever
tasted. there's no justice for him to die.
ground to push against: red earth,
bloody earth, stolen earth. what the pen
takes, the throat can return.

OUR SALT SPRING ISLAND DINNER

We invited the first and last words in postmodernism to our rebuttal, our Salt Spring Island dinner.

We cooked and served, they had to move their mouths fast to keep up. Foucault attacked discursive formations in the garlic mashed potatoes with his fork. Kristeva admitted the roasted carrots were too tender to be construed as phallocentric. Baudrillard crumbled up hyperreal simulacra and sprinkled it over his kale. Pass the bricolage, Barthes said.

Cumin and turmeric legends floated through the lamb curry, hinting at exotic intertextuality, a flaw in our argument perhaps. Fortunately, by that point, the blackberry wine had soaked Lacan's semiotics, making each morsel derivative of nothing but itself.

Everyone's body of work digested the reproof in the pudding differently. Derrida deconstructed himself in giggle fits. Barthes sung the song of the Swedish meta-chef. Saussure and Heidegger tried to do the dishes, but ended up running their foam-covered fingers through each other's moustaches.

Afterward, in the old orchard, we exhaled our education. Even the spiders spinning geometry could snare none of last century's fashionable nonsense as it exited our bodies in a puff of ganja, and vanished into the intelligent night. Our feline sentinel assumed her perch in the plum tree, on guard against any who would argue the full moon is not a perfect circle.

PARIS AT DUSK

Sunsets gather in a room
the size of an elevator,
waiting for their audition.
They parade past, one by one,
wearing red zebra-print dresses,
hats with iridescent feathers,
pink leg warmers that bunch
unflatteringly around the calf.
They sing in high, warbling voices,
overact, all daggers and tears,
do that same vanishing act,
hoping the director hasn't been dulled
to just another pretty face.

You bit a crepe hot from my hand
on a sidewalk narrow as a bicycle.
We fell into patio chairs
that belonged to no one,
held hands. On the wind,
veal bones stewed to melt, cigars,
butter like solace. The smooth oval
of the fountain pool rippled in dialogue
with our faces, then spread over the city,
painting all the buildings
the colour of a bruised plum.

Our sunset stood on stage
and made predictable choices:
monologue from Shakespeare,
lovers by a fountain in Paris.
Songbirds burst from her mouth,
cleaved the spotlight into *long purples,*
her clothes spread wide.
Then we remembered
why the bard is The Bard,
why we weep for Ophelia,
why the heart still shocks at the sky.

PELICAN

Ax in Greek, your bill would
bully wood. Dipped wingtip
to coast oceans that swallow miles
of oil & feathers. Maybe you
slipped under a shadow
pouch bulbous with whispers
that cut the air into crayfish.
Your cry pushes
a tugboat full of crustaceans
to boiling. How you love
to eat them! Was Mexico
a misplaced handshake
after God forgot to wash
the black out of blue
a distracted murmur at
the podium? Now nod
& vuln yourself raw before
the Eucharist, your blood
a forgotten promise, your
bill-pressed chest
a question mark.

POWER SAW ELEGY

Sandpaper time
Mill planed tree
Smelted ore
Pipelined fluids of the ground

Teenage workers of the world
Frolic in the affluent effluence
Drive mighty travel machines
To revel hard amid the distractions of growth

That drug be too strong
That car be too fast
That might be too many beers
To drink
To drive through a grove

Moloch trunk cathedral
Bearing crush
Cerebral impact

And my friend so-and-so
Who defies all opposite forces
If you listen
All you hear is no
To those who live young

Who in the light above the dashboard
Flew in a final futility
To fall finished
Upon the polished hoods and hard-tops

Victim and victor
Never old or contradicted
Blinded by idea
Enlightened by grief
Muddled by knowledge
Forsaken or remembered

PROUST AS IMPERATIVE

for Lisa Robertson

The rain. Sound & symbol of. The river Gar-
tempe is flowing in the distance. The signifier
of city plummets, torrents, pounds. Someone
in the distance, classify this under staccato. A
construction of we is underway. In bypassed
language, cleaning out, smoothing over, run
down memories demolished in lieu of shiny
baublefish in lieu of scales over littoral eyes.
We proust in the distance. At dusk could be
observed flocking toward the nearest proust.
Staging areas establish themselves. Narrative
is caught in collusion with scattergun truth
By morning, we are spattered white. Image
moved forward, moving forward, is shoved
down gullet like sea star after sea star. Prove
nature by algebra & stark frieze of succulent
proust. Raw & radioactive, slippery in gullet
is neither bulwark nor breakwater. To proust
off disaster, to proust ourselves off in shower
of circling image. The rain. Sound & symbol
of. In masterworks, in *chef doeuvre* & in rest
before clef we invert passionate tongues
we spit into crack of iconoclastic tract, into
hymenal idolatry post-epithalamion & at the
same moment we proust & proust & proust
we passerine twice–feel splendidly prousted.
Genuflect & pray for reprint the way cities
in the distance pray for rain. Pray for word-
fall, pray for fontlets of ink, annunciations
in wordleaf, tiny political icons in the shape
of patrons, words with the humanity of dry
fresco, finishing touches responding to air.
We are just waiting to cut into names with
paper knife, saving them for middle tome
for dog-eared ecstasies, for chichi spillage
for modish conceit, for conceptual yawn.
After ignominy & doom, after poetry was

strung up in a variety of styles, we enjoyed
ogling a quantity of poems, raining poems
that qualify for poemhood. French us, we
cried. French us, we cried & cried. Before
the recession, there was a light in the room
to read the people by. Reading the people
people rowing upon surface of a postcard
turning over in supply & demand of light
Depression was life of trauma & tantrum
reconfigured to lusky objective voice. We
the people are out of word, are prousting
off for the proust, with nowhere to proust
for the eventide, flowing in the distance. A
la recherche du temps perdu, in stone in the
middle of nowhere, near the river Gartempe.

RUSHING UNDERGROWTH

There is a robust grandeur, loud-voiced, springing richly from earth untilled,
unpampered, bursting forth rude, natural, without apology;
an awful force greater in its stillness than the crashing, pounding sea,
more akin to our own elements than water.
—Emily Carr, *Hundreds and Thousands*

It starts as a small voice, hum
caught in the back of the throat
a cough, accident of breath.
Walking becomes difficult
as the breath seeks a sister breath inside you.
You drop your own small stool,
your canvas where you stand, lower yourself
to the stool, closer to the chorus, closer
to the forces of the forest floor. Wait. Listen.
There is a robust grandeur, loud-voiced, springing richly from earth untilled.

You inhale, exhale
as the green forces glow clearer, lighter.
Around your feet green blood begins to boil.
Salal ripens before your eyes.
So few seek citizenship in this country.
Small animals come closer.
They wonder that you linger, a woman alone, unprotected by weapons.
Only the wooden brushes, lusty companions to your fingers.
No gun, no saw, no flame. How will you greet them,
unpampered, bursting forth rude, natural, without apology.

Others look for the familiar, desperate
for their own reflection. You sit, smoke, take your tea, your time.
Your skin fizzes with the hot and cold
of possibility. The dogs chase shadows.
It's a knowing-there's-something-there wait
'til it comes from behind announced
as a lift in the hairs on the back of your neck.
Rising damp, fierce tomtom of your blood.
At first you confuse it for your heartbeat then it is on you,
an awful force greater in its stillness than the crashing, pounding sea.

You seize the brushes as if they are oars
and pull for shore, staying barely ahead
of the shivery breath of undergrowth, trees
that rise and swell in a symphony of motion,
music to your eyes.
You are suspended in colour, now rising
through a hallelujah chorus of greens.
It breathes you, embraces you
this wet forest body
more akin to our own elements than water.

SHRINE FOR EVERY PART OF YOU

In discord

We can't be any other way

To break out of this house
you have to first break in

The holy ash scattered on the floor

Imagine a good argument

Now imagine the deepest blue of peace

In absence, waiting all day for night

In a cabinet with six farewell letters
In an oceanic bathtub
To wail over cards
To heal with water & sleep

Sympathetically
in our separate rooms
with forested bodies
& an eagerness for silence

SONG FOR THE DEAD

Your father in a hospital bed struggles for breath
and you wait on the line—long distance, can almost see
the phone on the nurse's desk on the other side of his room
But the cord won't reach.

You, across the country and why you and all your reasons ran from him
in the first place
doesn't matter anymore.

And you plead with the nurse, you beg her.
And she tells you again what you always knew, what you always feared—
he can't be moved towards you
and you hear yourself shouting, "Where the hell is fucking technology
haven't you heard of cordless phones—in that small minded town?"

Later, you imagine him putting his arms out towards you
and maybe he did, maybe he didn't
And you imagine he *will* call you when he gets better
but he doesn't
Because when it is the last time no one tells you.

So you take to wearing your father's sweater around the house,
Drink rum and coke from his coffee cup all day.
And in your dreams, you drive his station wagon too fast
slicing open the road like a knife thrown into the darkness.
The night air is a lunatic loose around you—
dances the ends of your hair, flaps the corners of clothing
as you race through time, trying to catch up with the past.

Fast as the red cars wild boys drive one-handed.
Those boys your father warned you about,
that you would one day take those dangerous rides with.
Fast as the stampede of trucks raging up from behind
that leaves you breathless and shaken, blind-sided,
wondering why you never saw his death coming.

You drive onward down the long highway
—an arrow into the broken heart of night.
Headlights search the dark stiffly, like bare white arms,

search for a way back home you no longer remember.
As the end plays over and over in your head,
how when the call came, it knocked the sky to the ground
brought you to your knees,
and all you remember is the woe of the dial tone.
This—the last sound love makes when it's dying.

STARING AT THE WINDOW IN THE PRIVATE FAMILY VISITING COTTAGE, WILLIAM HEAD PENITENTIARY, APRIL 2011

There has to be a flaw to perfect
the view, a smear
on the window at eye level
where a child has kissed
the reflection of his inquisitive lips.
If I looked beyond I could escape
into the wide sky that cannot stop
wild clouds from flying, but I can't
see further than this: the O
of his perfect mouth, my own pointless
lamenting. When I walk the dark road
to meet you, a stone lodges itself
inside my shoe: why don't I stop
to shake that pebble free?
It's as if we need the reminder, each step
of the way: it feels comforting, like an old
mother, the pain we obey.

STEALING ANATOMIES

In this slow time the physics of terror
are simple as a window. She is naked
when men push her through open frame.
The hair streams upwards — the formula
of her cry ricochets down brick walls.
Twisting: silk over alley. Shadows
engrave her nude back. Knives of light slash skin —
her angle is recalculated with each passing floor.

The dealers come to instruct, to inscribe
her in the streets. They begin with her body
and they will not finish. They toss out sneakers
as a coda. Understand this was not suicide.
Shoes rebound, hesitate, as if they
could. Men move through hallways
to streets, dispersing out of earshot.
A compression of red
stains the cement
where a coat is used to cover her.

Dabbing blood from her eyes, staunching
whispers; there is no time.
Faces from windows turn
towards her body, as satellites
track the moon. Ravens
untie from her hair.

Someone is stealing anatomies,
skin of fish, bones of bird.

TAI CHI, VAN DUSEN GARDENS

It's pawlownia season, finally
our Tai Chi world's gone wisteria-blue;
Keep heron-dancing.

Swinging slow before the huge Doug Firs we call home
maybe Muslim neighbours could use this too,
I wonder. Could they dig it? Just dancing?

Honkies need it too: meditation, a chance to pray in
each other's sacred courtyards.
Keep dancing!

At pawlownia time, everything is sacred here:
cool mornings, sun warming slowly.
It's a perfect time to enjoy your dancing.

We move and sway, the yellow perfume from *Pontia Azalea* sweet as
Hawaiian paradise,
it drifts our way: like dancing in Eden…

Hakuin Sensei got it all figured out: Eden is exactly this.
This very place *is* the Lotus Land. Please, everybody
Don't stop. Keep dancing!

Later, we stand and talk, delight in the garden view;
Fred worries, says nationalism is rising,
rising all around us.
In Thailand, Belgium, Quebec, Burma…
Amigos y amigas, S.V.P. keep on dancing!
Keep on dancing

In Brussels, a downtown corner, we pass sandbags—
conceptual art or a frontline warning?
Jitterbug around that machine-gun pit. Let's keep
dancing!

Vicious dogs, weapons—semiotics for dummies: "A failure to
Communicate" the Warden says in *Cool Hand Luke*.
I'd swear I heard Paul Newman from beyond the grave
smiling, tell us all,

Keep dancing

THE AUTOPSY REPORT

The deceased was found in his flying machine, slumped
by the side of the fairgrounds at approximately 8:34 AM.
He was cold as anyone is in this climate, but for him
the temperature had stabilized at minus 13 degrees and the snow
on his skin would no longer melt.
The morning sun, touching here on his cheekbones, there on the tip
of his nose, gilded him prettily but produced no waking effect.
Thus we bundled him into our carriage and proceeded to convey
him post-haste to the Hall of Turning Inside Out.
The deceased was a slender fellow with integuments fine
as handkerchiefs so that in one swift *shnitt* the chest
was opened like a letter, the entire cache of treasures bared.
Everything was there, I must reassure you, and more too besides,
for in trying to determine the time and cause of his flight, our delicate
instruments located a smouldering fire, a nest of bright feathers,
several violins, a grocery list with almost every item crossed off,
photos of a dog and one lock of night-dark hair.
It is not usual, I should tell you, to find such items at all,
never mind intact, a fact you might rejoice in despite your sorrow,
and beneath them was his heart, the cause of death, yes, when
at 5:42 the previous evening the organ overfilled itself with memories,
predominantly happy ones, but a few we've marked as regrets,
until the point of rupture was inevitable, bursting a hallway
between the chambers down which the deceased man quickly
walked, not looking back.

THE GOODNIGHT SKIRT

Permission to use that snowball
you've been keeping in the freezer
since 1998. For a poem? she asks.
What else? I say. I'll trade you, she says
for that thing your mom said
at the park. What was it?
God, that mallard's being a real son of a bitch?
Yes, that one. Deal, I say. Ok, how about
the young Korean boy that walks past
our house late at night, singing
Moon River? Oh, you can use that, I say,
I wouldn't even know what
to do with it. But there is something else.
I've been wanting to write about
the black skirt you've been using to cover
the lovebird's cage. The goodnight skirt.
In exchange, I'll let you have full coverage of
our drunken mailman, the tailless tabby cat,
and throw in the broken grandfather clock
we found in the forest. One more she says.
Last night, I say. The whole night.

She considers for a while, and then says
Ok, that's fair. But I really had something going
for that lovebird. Well, alright, I say, write it
anyway, if it's more beautiful than mine,
it's all yours.

THE NAMING OF PARTS

Used to be you took a pill,
it meant one thing.

Yesterday our odds and ends
didn't bend together. The week
before my gizmo didn't go
for your hoochamajigger.

All around us, youth
doing who-knows-what
with what-knows-where in
where-knows-how for
when-knows-how-long.

Doodads in oojamaflips.
Thingamajigs in whoseywhatsits.
In and out. Twenty-four hours
a day, seven days a week,
those kids with their caffeinated
drinks, pills and internets
bogging it down for their friends.

Used to be you took a pill,
it meant one thing.

Used to be in the war, I thought
of you as my one thing. Every time
we weren't having the blank bombed
out of us, I thought of touching you.
One day, one thought lead to another.
Had to right there in a rice paddy in Guam.
Eyes closed for you. Imagining
myself inside your you-know-what.
That's how I got the purple heart.
One minute my pants down for you
and the next some jibber-jabber, a bullet

in my leg and four months in a cell.
Prayed for a cyanide capsule to swallow.

But I wasn't a POW for internets or pills.
We fought for freedom of you-know-what
used to be.

THE NEXT GROWING SEASON: A GLOSSARY

Dimension: March, 2007
Sound: Trans-Canada Highway
Story: Abbotsford
Context: farming
Vehicle: tractor, transmitter, siren
Sound: churches, gurdwaras
Materials: baggy pants, tunic, scarves
Story: Amarjit Kaur Bal, 52
Exhibit: Killed
Valley: corn, cabbage-heads, water
Story : Sarbjit Kaur Sidhu, 31
Exhibit: Killed
Transaction: farm worker
Choice: organic
Materials: local
Field: Agro-chemical
Story: Abbotsford
Story: Sukhvinder Kaur Punia, 46
Exhibit: Killed
Sound: Trans-Canada Highway
Material: seatbelts
Un/authorized Interjection: March, 1914
Echo: "we want no interference with our labouring classes" ~ The Vancouver Sun
Material: farmer
Dimension: March, 2010
Sound: ceremony
Sadness: cherry blossoms
Valley: Amargit, Sarbjit, Sukhvinder
Broadcast: the correct pronunciation—*Abbotsferd,* not *Abbotsford*
Field: mother, daughter, aunt
Sound: grandfather, daughter, cousin
Object: 3 photographs. 1 memorial
Subject: their story, their story, their story
Time: and its dimensions

THE STONE

They never asked me
For my name
They wanted my identity card
Or its number

I did not have one

I said Stone

They laughed
Asked me where I was from

From the stone—I said

They asked for my age

Twenty pebbles—I answered
And showed them greyspotted-pebbles

They are opening their hearts to me
I am closing the doorway on the invisible wall
Which divides us
And I am going away

THE WAILING MACHINES

I wanted to say: look, this intersection, this place
where we have come together and stopped traffic,
is the only place we ever could have met, you and I—
pistons that never before aligned, even when the engine
was at rest, that had to wait until the whole contraption
burst and we were spilled out onto the pavement to see that yes,
all those hints—those darting noises, glints of steam and light—
held truth, that there are others as startled and ragged as ourselves,
and somehow gaining that knowledge seems worth all this blood
and bother and traffic lined up over the crest of the hill.
I wanted to say all of this, but my throat sputtered
which is why I merely waved as we were lifted away
and placed inside the wailing machines
we were only beginning to know to imagine.

THE WEIGHT OF DEW

can I fill these words with what is not
intended.   with what the river keeps

hidden
                    under her tongue.

with the maps birds carve in my marrow
fill my bones   with air

my eye   with their dying.

to wait on the river bank
                              long enough

to know what knowing   looks like
before   it is disturbed.

stepped on.   sanitized.
poked   with a stick.
put   in a vial.

to know the shape of   me

nameless—   my given names left out
like shoes   I was meant to fill.

they gather dew   now

it slides down their tongues. I watch them
through this open door   where

even the clock   wipes its face clean.

THE WINE DARK SEA

1
He held a gallon jar above his head
Graceful as an Olympic diver at five he dove,
hands and jar extended,
from the top of the cement barbeque
to the sea of patio concrete below
and scalped himself.
So when mom took the tea towel
and wiped the blood from his forehead
all his hair lifted up
like an insecure toupee.

Of course mom screamed a lot and
it took a doctor twenty stitches
to sew the stuffing
back into his head.

2
When he was eight years old
and culpable before the Mormon god,
they decided to baptize his abnormally long body
by full immersion for the remission of his sins.

Each time they tried, plunging him under,
a toe or finger or elbow would refuse to submerge.

For years after he was a joke with the local congregation
holding the record for the number of times
dunked before they got him right under, completely immersed,
in another place with gravity suspended.

3
When he was about five he would wander off
whenever I was assigned to look after him.

One day in a blustery late November I had taken
him to the long beach by Semiahmoo Bay.
I recall our large puffy parkas, mitts, boots.

Distracted by birds or agates or whips of seaweed
I forgot about him and when I looked he was knee deep
in the wine dark sea.
And then he was waist deep and then neck deep and then submerged.
But every few seconds his head
would burst through the surface
blowing like a whale and then down
and relentlessly forward he'd go until
I caught up with him and dragged him blubbering to shore.

Then one day,
years later, he suspended his tall frame
in too short a room and defied gravity like
a fish on a string,
received a remission of sin,
entered the gallon jar with one smooth cartoon move,
took an endless hike on the beach
at the bottom of Semiahmoo Bay.

TONGUE

Wrap your tongue around me and tell me a story. Your words slip
Like liquor down the back of my throat. I love to watch your mouth move
And I wonder what it tastes like. Can I stare? Can I brush against you
Like a slow accident? Can I stare? Can I stare with my hands,
with my mouth,
with my tongue?
'Cause there is a creamy sweetness here that is richer deeper better than
the best sugarbuttercookiebatterbowl that I have ever licked. (Suck
these sticky fingers dry.) I bet you taste
like a pomegranate. I bet you'd leave stains like bruises
on my lips. I bet you'd have freckles if I stood close enough. I bet you
know secrets you'll never tell. I bet you smell like autumn leaves. I bet
your skin has scars so fine only my tongue can see them:
not my eyes,
not my hands. I bet you taste
nothing like grapefruit. I bet when you wake into the morning
and stretch and turn over there's a place on your back by your
shoulder
blade where the skin ripples and dimples into fantasy.
You are more than mere geometry, biology, random spasms of electricity.
Your hands —your hands!— can only be described in terms of
theology. You are dancing like a human being shaking as though
God Himself invented you. You are bigger than your own bones.
You are so small you are eclipsed by the weight
of your own breath. I bet your skin tells stories
only your lovers hear. I bet you have tattoos. I bet you barely
remember getting them.
I bet there's a name someplace quiet like the curve of your foot.
I bet there's a story there of you and her. I bet you keep bruises
on your knees like pets. I bet you taste like cigarettes. If I could curl
my body 'round the curve of your back, like you curve your words
down the back of your throat, as smoke curls between your fingers,
surely I could live forever or at least live surely.
Wrap your tongue around me
and tell me.

WHAT WE HEARD ABOUT THE CANADIANS

We heard they were not American.
Not British and not quite French.

They were not born in Hong Kong
did not immigrate from Russia with one pair of shoes.

They were not all russet-haired orphans
who greeted the apple blossom dawn with open arms,

crying *Avonlea!* They were not immodest,
did not want God to save the Queen.

Their leaders were not corrupt, no;
they were not all Mounties on proud horseback

with hot tasers. *Fuck me* was not considered impolite
in their living rooms.

It was not just the weather that made them curse.
Not just frozen lakes cracked under the weight of the moon,

There was no great Canadian hush of things not to be talked about.
Not all of them ignored genocide.

Not all of them sang a "cold
and broken Hallelujah" as the bells broke crystal ice

across Parc Lafontaine. They were not rich and also
not poor. Not overachievers. Neither believers nor unbelievers.

C'etait pas tout l'histoire, and they would not
be caught clubbing seals on TV, red bloom

on white coat, melting eyes, they did not mine asbestos
in Quebec, make love in skidoos,

sleep in snowshoes. Never danced hatless

under dancing northern lights. They were polite.

WORDSONG

remembering Miki

Adib Adele
abed a bell

a star Estelle
alas too far

aslant afoot
a door ajar

akin alike
a three-wheeled bike

or nothing more
than Western Shrike

a thing so true
as morning light

a boat ashore
a bird in flight

this August day
a soul astray

YOU GO TO TOWN

We'll okay demo of
trees, bushes if once you're finished
building your condo
condo condo condo condo
condo condo condo condo
condo townhouse condo condo
condo condo condo condo
you'll lay cement form
sidewalks trim edges snuggle blankets
of grass. You see,
we didn't have sidewalks before
just ditches.

It's okay to set sale,
labour identity over
website over press release over
word-of-mouth if once you've
broken
soil you barrier
the big tree and take care not to
accidentally, an accident,
kill roots.

Seattle

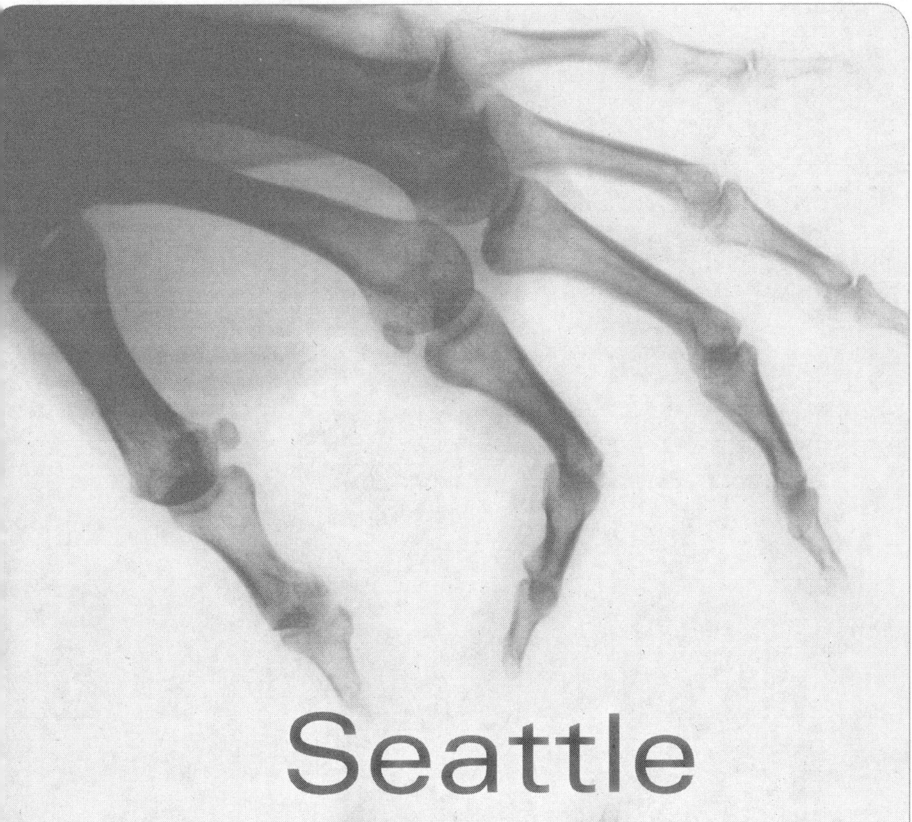

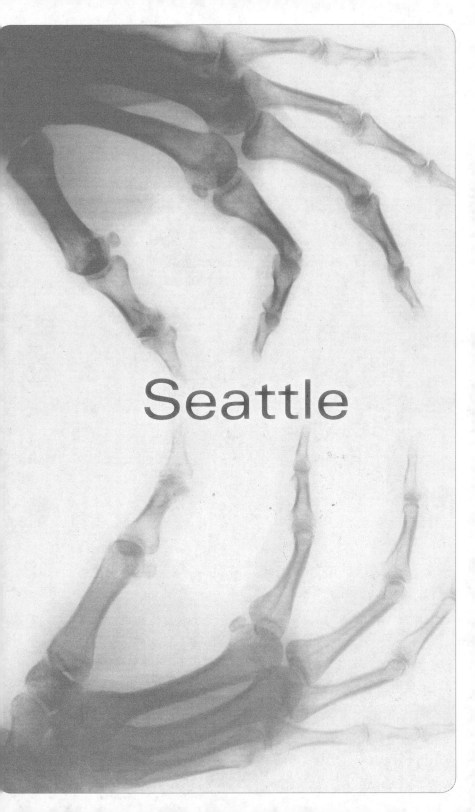

POEMS FROM SEATTLE, WASHINGTON

In "A Backward Glance o'er Travel'd Roads," Walt Whitman imagined a future for his poems: "Henceforth, if they live and are read, it must be just as much South as North—just as much along the Pacific as Atlantic—in the valley of the Mississippi, in Canada, up in Maine, down in Texas, and on the shores of Puget Sound." Whitman proved prescient, as ever—and how lovely to think of him thinking of us, as we encounter him a century and a half later, in this Northwest outpost. (Though he predicted that, too. From "Crossing Brooklyn Ferry": "What is it then between us? / What is the count of the scores or hundreds of years between us? // Whatever it is, it avails not—distance avails not, and place avails not.")

Among the readers Whitman predicted, many are also writers: testers of rhyme and unreason, in the shadow of Rainier. And while I'm reluctant to make grand claims for regional poetry (shared orbits of influence strike me as more significant than, say, a shared landscape), an inescapable fact remains: somehow, someway, in busy and beautiful Seattle, we've wound up with more than our share of permanent (or potentially permanent) poets. Why?

I blame the bookstores, in part: Elliott Bay Book Company, Third Place Books, and, especially, Open Books, the poetry-only emporium that serves as a kind of headquarters for Seattle scribes. I blame the University of Washington, with its mind-expanding MFA program and its faculty of crazy geniuses (many certifiably so: think MacArthur, not McLean). I blame the Richard Hugo House, with its Cheap Wine and Poetry nights and, for those under twenty-one, a wealth of after-school classes and summer programs. I blame Seattle Arts & Lectures, which not only brings world-class poets to town for readings and interviews, but also administers the spectacular Writers in the Schools program that exposes thousands of students each year to poetry's world of real toads and imaginary gardens.

What I'm describing, of course, is a literary culture. Other contributors to that culture include the region's vibrant journals (*Poetry Northwest, Filter, Crab Creek Review, The Seattle Review*); presses (Floating Bridge, Wave Books, Rose Alley), and performance groups (Seattle Poetry Slam, Youth Speaks); *The Stranger's* Books section; the literary programming on KUOW; and the City Council's support of the arts. (What other city would've allowed someone—OK, me—to open a council session with a poem called "Bozo Sapphics?") Poets may not be Seattle's unacknowledged legislators, but they play an important role in its identity. In this rough-weather town, we have poetry stuffed in our parkas and stashed under our boot-soles.

I'm enormously indebted to Kathleen Flenniken and David Horowitz for unearthing poets and poems new to me, as well as for championing work by many of my favorite Seattle writers. Both Kathleen and David's generosity and discernment were invaluable in shaping this collection. If I have a bias when it comes to making anthology selections, it's against poems that feel, to me, as if they were written with two hands: one hand doing the writing, the other hand patting the writer's own back. So you won't find self-congratulatory epiphanies in the pages that follow. (In David Mitchell's *Black Swan Green,* the heroic Madame Crommelynck addresses such a poem: "It says, 'Am I not a pretty pretty?' I answer, 'Go to the hell!'") What you'll find instead is an array of poems that challenge our preconceptions, including those of what a poem may be. The poems are blunt, tuneful, and, finally, mysterious—in the way of all things that merit our reflection.

Whitman's "Backward Glance" ends, famously: "The strongest and sweetest songs yet remain to be sung." That may always be true; it gives us something to hope for, anyway. Still, I like to think that some of those lasting carols are being sung today on the shores of Puget Sound. It's a strange kind of music; I can't get it out of my head.

—*Cody Walker*

A POEM BY BRIAN MCGUIGAN

My mother wanted to name me hardworking peasant.
Grandma said no. How about a good Irish name?
A roughhousing round earth name, she said.
My mother wanted to name me Fuck you, man.
Or Remington. But Grandma said no.
I was like two dogs at the park.
I pounced on my hand, bit myself
and bled like crazy. Often
I tell people I'm in a gang
but it's just me.
My skin is a secret shade
of dirt. My cat had more eyes
than teeth, pulled grass the dog
pissed on, did not allow holding.
My mother wanted boys
to have vaginas.
Poetry is the opposite of giving my mother
what she wants.
No holding is a rotten rule.
Fuck you, man.
My mother named me Tammy.
Call me hardworking. Call me
Brian. Hold me
to it. My name
means the earth is round.

ABLATION AS THE CREATION OF ADAM

The world is always beginning.
A face sweeps over in the vertigo of anesthesia.

A light gauze or a saline wash…something to ease me
into this century tells me about the first darkness.

In the beginning, there was a whole me. There was
an end I could not see. And there were sounds—a siren

set the hounds off. In between crickets, a radio.
And between the radio, the hush of a respirator.

The aurora of the surgical lamp formed blue rings
behind shut eyes. Let there be and there was…gossamer thin,

the numbed pulse. Pulse, the memory of the heart.
Heart, the now-tongue. The here-flower.

Useless is the thing taken out of the body. Little stinkweed.
Little broken thrush. What's left—a socket. A keyhole.

I used to have something to miss, now my neck's a rattletrap.
Thus my body was corrected. A hand moved the waters

and said flesh be done. And it was done. Evening.
Morning. The sterile tube shunted into my neck.

And it was good. I rose, fawn-weary. The stun of spiced cleaner
cooled the room. Nothing like the clean of a new world

with my new none-body. My "hardly notice."
A new clock is wound behind the curtain.

The cut is now a blush. Apoplectic ravine. Cave scrawl.
My zippered nest. Pink ellipsis, I shall name you, my flamingo.

Somewhere, birds rise above the African coast like blown tissue.
The volcanic sun silhouettes their wings as they lift off. Then, the dizzy
horizon.

AFTERNOON ABOVE I-5

We used to drop acid
and sit on the overpass
to watch the dragon faces
the cars would make at us
as they raced
beneath our dangling legs.
Cars like it when you're high enough
above them to notice
more than their surfaces.
It's the story of their exhaust
they want you to care about,
not their paint jobs
or the treads
on their tires. They want you to lean down
and touch them.
I know what you're thinking.
It's dangerous,
what we used to do. But
the cars told us they'd catch us if we fell.
You say, *So what if they did?*
And you're right.
There's always a catch.

Jeremy Halinen

ALARIC INTELLIGENCE MEMO #36

Their women are whores; their men are boys,
Stalled to inertia by infinite choice.
They live in a hell of marvels: fierce,
Fully automated joys.

The prowess of their engineers
Is justly fabled. They've leapt to the nearest
Lamps of night. Such chasms spanned!—
Too black for all but their blindest seers.

Their warrior class, insufficiently manned,
Is mad, responsive, and under command.
Their weapon of choice is the toggle switch.
Be watchful. They kill with either hand.

They diddle themselves to a sexual scorch
From middle childhood through advanced age,
To worship the Mother, conceptualized
As a green severity bearing a torch.

Their gods are tripe, cradled inside,
Served by a priesthood garbed in white
Who sometimes remove them with sharpened spoons,
And cast them away. I cannot say why.

Their poetry barks. Their faith, a ruin,
Ghost-infested, affords no womb
Of future. In sum: however skilled,
They are overripe. My Lord, strike soon.

Addendum: proud to have served your will,
I have lived too long among them. I am ill.
I am infected with dreams. At the first moon
Of conquest, I respectfully request to be killed.

Herewith committed to blood rune
By Agent 36, without witness or wergild
This first Sunday of the Tooth Month,
Praise God, of God's Year One.

AUGURIES

1. Gods Wrought

And another thing, Professor: if Heaven is
A field generated by neurology,
And gods are seen as knots or local disturbances

Of the field, doesn't the sheer evanescence
Of it horrify first? Wouldn't raw logic
Require it all to flicker, should the turbines

Fail and whirr down? *Then wink out?* The nonsense
Verse and husky stonepiles of Religion
All that's left, their casketry.... The gods, on pins

And needles, must suspect this. Excitation in the xenon
Tube! Wave functions collapsing throughout the Elysian
Field! Noses pressed to the police-glass of penance:

Insentient they may be; that doesn't make them stupid.<
Gods must watch augurs slit live birds, too.

2. Augur Gone

But what if our augurs, scratching at the new,
Whatever that is, should watch by auspices
Some bird-speck up the sweep of the long blue
Resolve again into a *god?*—waspish,

Close-clung, driving the filed spurs
Of his intention home into the future
Through the tissue of the breast?—To pierce
The veil of the real again!—that would be virtue

In its root sense. No flickery hologram,
But Man, knee deep in the magma pool of dawn
Again, bleeding out imaginary grammars
Hot enough to speak what eidolons

We dream: gods again, not numbers numbing
Heaven to a thought, but *real gods* again, or coming.

BLOOMERY

We made a furnace of dirt
threw dirt in
when it was done dug dirt out

dirt necklace dirt needle
dirt knife dirt bone
dirt button dirt pot

dirt babies
crying dirt cries
we fed them dirt milk

wrapped them warm in dirt blankets
boiled dirt kettles
to keep their dirt diapers clean

on their dirt birthdays
gave them dirt bears
dirt bedtime read them dirt geese

when they left for dirt school
dirt grammar dirt math
dirt art dirt lunch

we wrote in our dirt journal
dirt alone at the dirt kitchen table
each day another dirt day

at their dirt weddings
dirt cake dirt fizz
and home to our own dirt bed

when we were dirt old
we locked our dirt house
and went to the forest

dug a dirt furnace
climbed in
until dirt was done

BOONDOCKS

We come from there—that
clattering tautology. The boon's

the boom—what lowers a load
from the tottering sky;

the dock's the planks and pilings,
strictness of the structures made

so we can walk on water, put
these franking footholds on

the riled-up rookery; the dock's
the bracing that the boat is lashed to:

tarry trunk, and tacky creosote.
An orange star attaches to a moment,

waves toward a slo-mo lobe.
A finger's inch outruns

a yardarm's reach—the boon's
the rope, the slip, the pilings, and

the sound. We come from there,
and we want more. Another ton

of sky-stuff winches down.

CLOSET VISION

Holed up behind the whitewashed wooden slats
slung like ribs above the greed-begotten candy, plaster
papered Now-And-Laters, holed up and far
from witches in the woods' evergreen fringe,
horse chestnut brews, parents' crow commotion or
robin squabble haranguing the fat
wide open always out there, I read for hours
on the red shag rug hearing market cry
and grave slope, caught the men through ages
of flint and full haggle in my two-by-six chamber,
my heart hooked on Bluebeard and the dead wives'
skeletons cantilevered to a door hook. Later,
hunkered down with amputee hangers,
catalogs, the bottle stash and jug wines,
Jim Beams too hiding with air, no air,
plus a stolen *Joy of Sex* circa 1974,
its pell-mell positions and crouching
women, with the POV going scrape and rattle,
some theater of being a little less bright.
Saw one night the million paired eyes
swinging upward, the hand-me-down generations
spelunking in caves, fine lineaments braved
by way of cream curd and lust and dictatorial DNA,
felt through overhead squib and carpet warp,
some full squat before the slate rock hearths,
more buried in strata of granite, igneous,
limestone, ash, the mind's eye leveled
to one rectangle of light around the animal
who wants to know that it knows and say so,
lumbering down a long path to vanishing.

COMMUTE

The evening's amber alert lights up.
Modern sunset, another abduction,

and fuck, traffic is bad. The girl
in the next lane texts while driving,

her mouth like the knotted pucker
of a helium balloon. Everything electric blows

eventually: light bulbs, crushes, what have you.
Even *dynamite* has fizzled to *super.*

Annually, too many people at a party
crowd a lanai and it gives way the way

one day relents to the next.
This summer's collapse is coming up.

I commute but am not moved. *That jerk.*
Sometimes I touch a nerve to see if it still works.

CRUSADE

When my friend and I dug a ten-foot-deep hole in a baseball field, I remembered a magazine article that compared two men fucking the same woman to digging a hole with complete concentration, neither guy looking at the other's shovel. The night we fucked the same woman, I woke up at 3 am and watched her sleeping between us. My friend slept turned to the wall. I thought of the things underground that no one existing had touched: bones, jars, porcelain dolls' legs, the unbroken bottle we held and looked at so carefully as the maintenance guy on his lawnmower roared through the sunlight above us.

DOUBLE ABECEDARIAN: PLEASE GIVE ME

Anything and anybody but Freud, that Bic-and-Pez-
Bitten, cylinder-obsessed, Big-Cigar-as-Envy
Calamity of a man who posited the idea that sex
Dachshund-style with Mom might possibly show
Evidence of a troubled mind. How did every concave *V*
Female its way into his convex psyche? *Mon dieu,*
Gott im himmel, por el amor de dios—just one night
How I'd like to translate myself without the shrinks.
I wouldn't get lost in fog, I wouldn't be a beggar
Jumping off the *Pont Neuf,* wouldn't be a twisted *Q*
Knocking up some *U* with my tail, nor a Lap-
Lander hitching myself to my own sled. No,
More likely I'd just be sitting looking for a reason
Not to stop sitting. There'd either be me in this dream,
Or some smoke and some midgets. Does all hell
Position itself for a couched session with that sick
Quill-and-quiver-addled Viennese? He's still the Raj
Royale of our subsurfaces, isn't he, the Rabbi
Sigmund ben Oedipus? He makes even bowls of mush
Turn into latent tendencies, while we keep cranking
Up his sirens without any downtime or relief.
Virility as a red fire hydrant, lust as a long flagpole?
Where on this earth, or where off it, do these bad
X-rated verticalities escape from his narrative arc?
Yes, the shapes of this world go from arrow to orb,
Zero is a pierced hole. But what a lot of hoopla.

ESTRANGEMENT IN ATHENS

Mount Olympus held nothing for them.
No occasion of theirs could provoke
Magniloquent debate. Nor act require
That attic of gods to come swooping
Onto the field, swaying the battle.
Only the great booming of the ferry
As it shouldered alongside the pier;
Only the waitress counting their
Saucers; it was this April morning
That swung them by their heels.
What was missing was the impersonal,
The fated, a visionary marble address,
The goddess skimming over blue water
To whisper good news, or some stud,
Swan, or bull brimming with light.
Not a wingéd foot. Only Love,
Recently decamped, hovered above
The table, ready to be splendid.
But their ten years' war had ended.

FIRST CHANTEY

From tumbled star shine
once upon a time
and the stethoscope's echo,
calendar pages punched confetti,
from the submarine jelly roll
periscope view into
mare nostrum's water ballet,
from the caged sashay of a winged elbow
from the dark swan dive,
fists first squinting at the surface glare,
from the close-reefed sails
in a broad reach,
and the wind's red wail relenting,
to you, becalmed at last,
latched at the mooring of a milky sea.

FISHING SCENE

We lie like a married couple
on a couch, watching a movie—
from the screen a couple passes us the rig
so we can feel the monster on the line,
but our wrists are too weak to divide
the fish from its dive.

They laugh, take over,
no questions asked.
In a few frenzied gestures,
they land it, curse its girth,
club it, gut it,
cut out its heart to impress us—
look, the heart keeps beating
without its fish!

We stand in gore—
the wind comments on our stale smell,
blood unfurls like fern fronds
in a few inches of salt water,
pink entrails float across our boots,
scales shed in lavender wafers,
silver confetti all over the red deck,
the carcass a reliquary,
one dim eye a vial of clouds
muzzling the sky.
We stare over the side,
gray waves drumming.

One screen-ghost called out to me,
"Bear with me, I lived life—
foolishly." We lie like a married couple
touching each other to get well,
couched in red, pink, lavender,
green, and silver.
Later the other passed on
the advice, "Feast on color!"

FROM THE TOWER

Insanity is not a want of reason.
It is reason's overgrowth, a calculating kudzu.
Explaining why, in two-ton *manifesti,* thinkers sally forth
with testaments and pipe bombs. Heaven help us:

spare us all your meaningful designs. Shine
down or shower forth, but for our earthling sakes
ignore all prayers followed by *against,* or *for*.
Teach us to bear life's senselessness, and our

own insignificance. Let's call that sanity.
The terrifying prospect isn't some poor
sucker in a La-Z-Boy, inclined to jokes,
remotes, or sweets. It is the busy hermeneut,

so serious he's sour, intent on making
meaning of us all—

and bursting from the tower to the streets.

HIDDEN

Hidden
as a toy balloon in the sky is
and is not
As a hawk in the sky
over a pasture
is and is not
What is hidden
like what is beautiful
is in the eye
You may be a thing
stained with tinctures
and packeted in muslin
and tinkered up in a small balsa box
and set on a root-cellar shelf
But you are not hidden
unless someone seeks you
and does not know you are
a thing dyed by walnut shells
that has been wrapped
in a saved sheet of tinfoil
and folded into the pocket square
of a discarded apron
and closed inside a jumble drawer

HISTORY OF PARANOIA

The self-administered questionnaire meant to identify Martians produces frequent false positives: the English, rural Canadians, anyone raised without a television. Talking horses. False negatives could be happening just as frequently, it's hard to know. There's no other way of identifying the Martians, it's only this take-home exam with the stamped pre-addressed envelope. Most everyone could be a false negative, and eyeing us, and reading our minds, and nightly de-tentacling. As with other tests designed by this service, and fairy tales, and much of adult life in general, there have been no true positives.

HISTORY OF TRANSLATION

The joke "How many surrealists does it take to change a light bulb?" becomes, in German, "How many surrealists—the answer, by the way, is fish—does it take to change a light bulb? Fish, yes, that's correct. Sehr gut."

HOMETOWN (A SAVIOR SAVES BY NOT SAVING)

who might—to might—give out a kindness
to weakness, pay out a kindness

Through our covered bridge
Scatter-Love Abiding, come

over loose boards with slits of the river
Scatter-Love Abiding, come
with Your slow face
and Your empty hands

unshocked by August out the other side
sex of sky, nothing swollen like we

under the tree shimmer
and over popping tar

come

though
Smudged Glasses wants else than this
and Daylily Heart wants this and more
and who is hair-twirly sad and sour?
O gritty citizen longing

let kindness
that is Cold-Love Abiding
walk maple-nut scattered
unto the tattery edges of this town

out the bridge mouth
come unpuzzled this
Particle-Love Abiding

HONEYMOON

Suppose you know your friends
have been together for five years
without ever having sex, and then

they marry, even the words *we're enjoying*
the toaster seem scorched onto the thank-you note,
seem frenzied with innuendo.

And there they are, up against
the kitchen counter of your mind,
the settings twisted to dark,

burnt bread panting out hotly from the two slots
like twin beds aflame, a jar of something sweet
tipped and spilling a slow motion stream

to the tile. Perhaps it is not how you would do it,
but it makes sense, how they did it:
the wedding in the Midwest,

the land like a sheet, one corn-colored mile
unfolding after another. The honeymooning
not in Greece or *Paree*

but at home, all things being new
and sharp as untried registry knives
Imagine the bear

standing before that at-long-last hive,
how he's all skin and bones
from living so long

on just nuts and berries.
Listen for the bees of *yes*
and *no* and *not yet*

swarming sleepy, subdued from the smoke
of the fire just lit. Above, the hunger
moon grows to overflowing.

And the first taste—
the condensed collection, the work,
the wait, the intricate dance

of all those years—
tastes sweeter taken straight
from the paw.

HUMANS

a brief and strange species
—W. S. Merwin

the day begins in disarray *you ought you should you must*
you must you must you must the bees will not

be stilled what stitches mind to body who cues the unraveling
if it's true we're infused with something not found in doorknob bird or
bee

why am I confused about all the important things crows
trampoline the power lines from house to house they don't care

who runs the world I gape at the skycolor of sunflower
color of blood the world is not as I have believed it to be

I find no vantage point no long view across even the surface
peristalsis propels the worm into darkness electricity

animates the lamp the leaf drinks at the top of the tree
I understand none of the beautiful things the sparrow bathes

in dirt I don't know why the birds do not ask themselves
or each other how are we to live they do not ask us to love them

HUSBAND, WIFE

He resembles a small star, composed
of rapidly spinning light,
and strong east-west winds.
The pressure inside him has a faint ring,
flattened and cloud-like, which
is actually debris from the interior
caused by slow compression.
He swims in the form of a swan.

She is larger, more than twice the mass
of everything else put together. A giant.
A storm system that has raged for years.
She radiates more energy into space
than she receives from the sun.
The fact that she is big enough to hold
two earths makes it difficult to distinguish
between her atmosphere and her surface.

Husband, wife: no one knows
how such structures can survive.

I TAKE THE SAME WAY ALMOST EVERY DAY.

12.

I take it
    or I say so, standing
here: in the alley between mansions
and more, braced on a sag in the staircase to the garden
of a house without a door.

No door means nothing
but the steps are kin to a different set
behind a church on a hill
above Rome.

            (Here
I am attempting
to say something
about privacy

as in,

my thought
still sits where I stopped it
on the cement twist
of a turning set
of descending steps
behind a church
on a hill
above Rome
while in my mind
I come shyly from behind
to trespass on a yard in Seattle.)

If we had a privacy contest I would win it.
In other words, no door.

IN OTHER NEWS

I'm not going to call the painter crazy if he sees the Virgin
in a prostitute. Now is not the Counter-Reformation.

Now is postmodernism. The liberation forces have left altars
standing in the open. Every time you win the war

you learn another way not to win the war. Poets still write
books to be published "before our death

instead of when death comes." Look at the snowfall, the light
dust on the broken wall. Watch the tragic actor

closely, and he becomes hysterical. Somewhere on the radio
a first time caller describes the Lord on toast;

she's capable of paying close attention. Fifteen seconds max.
Are you Margaret, God? It's me, Johnny,

and I'm looking for an easy way out. Love Is A Dog From Hell,
Bukowski wrote, and look what he got:

an army of undergraduates who confuse dorm life with poverty.
No one cursed the one room schoolhouse

like your mother, who once said Victor Hugo was American.
Avoid shacking up with your English professor

became the standard warning. Avoid living between paychecks
with a bare-knuckle boxer. In Bernini's Ecstasy

of St. Theresa, ancillary figures look a lot like the Inquisition
unless you're already thinking about reality

television. Tell me a celebrity judge can distinguish an orgasm
from divine intervention. What about fire-

tipped arrows going straight for your privates? Fuck that noise.
I'm learning via satellite about the orangutan

who made harmonicas out of grass. It doesn't sound scientific
if you say Australopithecus invented music

as a trick to frighten hyenas; and yet, bartenders across America
crank the worst songs at closing time:

We had joy; we had fun; we had seasons in the sun, but stars
we could reach were just starfish

on the beach. Take me out and I'll teach you a lesson: snow
globes; a telescope; stars that burnt out

long before troglodytes first rubbed sticks. I've been watching
the Weather Channel for the latest crisis.

Someone's getting stuck in holiday traffic. I have a hula dancer
just in case you've lost your dashboard Jesus.

KING LIMBO

A dowel between notched poles is set
a neat six inches from the grass.
This is the gate to Limbo, through which
 a full grown man must pass,

A black man, lean and sinewy,
his forearms roped with vein like vine,
in an emerald cape with silver plumes,
 Haitian in design.

He lifts a sequined kettle high
against blue sky without a cloud.
One hand unfurls a five to nudge
 the stingy Ballard crowd.

He passes this collection plate,
we glimpse his few chest hairs arrayed
like the rays a magnet makes in dust,
 his floppy slippers, frayed.

He bends to kiss *The Guinness Book*
of World Records, bible of renown.
It gives the history of his reign,
 each challenge to his crown.

Lamp oil lit, he sets ablaze
the margin under which he'll squeeze.
To get a camel through a needle,
 first bring it to its knees.

As if it weren't impossible,
he threads his body through the portal,
and rises on the other side,
 in tear-stung eyes, immortal,

And if we paid, or didn't pay,
either way, it gives us chills.
I toss my small change on a kettle
 overflowing bills.

KINSHIP

We stretched our feathers
over each other, and then
across the foundling child.
She was without. No wings,
not from where she came.
We took her in and made
her part of this world without
loft and cloud. We crawled
up on either side of her;
we spread our wings
tip-to-tip and tucked the girl's
little face beneath.
Amidst the humming
song of the hand-cranked,
cable-round-the-gear,
squeak and thimble melody,
we winged her: fragile girl,
beloved child. Ours.

LAST OF SPRING

On June the twenty-first, just after noon,
the sun shines down a city alleyway,
all other days occult and garbage strewn
but briefly bathed in light this solstice day.

With endless labor ancient engineers
aligned their monuments to calculate
the holy turns and terminals of years
that no one comes here now to celebrate.

The year-around, though, warehouse workers use
their hour at lunch to shoot some hoops
among the gutters' green and greasy ooze,
the dented garbage cans, the grimy stoops.

Today they're playing in a different light,
a luminosity that gives their game
an unaccustomed lightness, almost flight,
and seems to set the concrete world aflame.

The shadows rise first waist-, then shoulder-high;
the players' time grows short, they pass and run—
they spring beneath their narrow strip of sky
to catch the ball, as if to catch the sun.

MAGNOLIA BLOSSOM

Who knew so many shades of white
could exist in one blossom?
Popcorn and sourdough,
bleached jean and sand.
All the satiny tones of wedding dress
and mayonnaise, cuticle and tusk.
And rising from the dizzying
whirl of snowy petals
a swollen, clitoral seed tower
all breadfruit and ivory,
sticky as shredded coconut.
They say white is not the absence
of color, but its fullness.
A painter's box laden with pearl necklace,
cigarette smoke, bone china, milk.
Cloudbank and table linen,
oyster shell, starlight.

MAN IN THE STREET

He claps a hand
Across the gaping hole—

Or else the sight
Might well inside to

Melt the mind—if any
Thinking spoke

Were in the wheel,
Or any real

Fright-fragments broke
Out of the gorge to

Soak the breast, the meaning might
Incite a stroke. Best

Press against it, close
The clawhole, stand

In stupor, petrified. The dream
Be damned, the deeps defied.

(The hand's to keep
The scream inside.)

MONSTER

Even the wet floor of the city bus, that slimy
torso, muddy with mountain spit, challenging each
rider's ankle to a duel, is romantic on an April afternoon.

I board in West Seattle, cross the bridge beneath
the eye of a volcano, pray an earthquake
doesn't come while we're on the viaduct,
sled the exit ramp into downtown, when
suddenly the bus driver stands on his brakes!

Rearing up on her hind legs in front of the bus,
two feet planted in the Puget Sound, yellow claws
tapping the tops of skyscrapers, stands Spring:

Godzilla with a head full of flowers, Gorgon with ivy
for snakes. She sniffs the bus, then sneezes, licks every tree twice.
She shoves her face in the ocean, shakes her dragon head in a pink fury;
rhododendrons rain over First Avenue.

The driver, terrified, turns up Pike, steps on the gas. We spill
our purses, fall into each other's laps. He knows Spring wants
to eat us like fat chickens, sucking the grease from our bones.
She wants to snap our spines before tossing us skulls first into
Summer. "Take them," she rages at her cousin-season. "They
always liked you better."

Monster of an adolescent girl,
Spring turns thirteen every year. She coats the city
in cherry blossoms so it will look like her messy bedroom,
laundry on the floor and phone ringing. She tosses punches filled
with pollen and wails, "I know that slut Summer is coming
with her long legs and her easy love." Spring cries now and all the
hydrants on Pine Street explode, starts stomping up the staircase
of the city, "Mom, have you seen my sunglasses?" "Mom, I can't find my
flip-flops!"
She hates the color brown, hates boring things, loathes the way everyone
waits for Summer with her brown skin and her pink blush. "I'm good
enough,"
she sobs into the clouds. "If you loved me like you should love me,
I would stay here all year."

Spring's tears fall off and coat the bus like oil,
where they splash on the concrete moss and mushrooms
grow. She straightens up and steadies herself,
shakes out her hair and unclenches her hands. Tulips
fill the flowerbeds. When she leaves us, she goes
back to the ocean, through the Puget Sound.
Only the magnolia trees go with her.

MY NEW LIFE

I'll start it after lunch.

Maybe staring at the mountain
will encourage it,

twinkle of someone's dropped
watch in a crack.

How dewy, washed, transparent all will be then,
how musical, rilling and coursing.

And yet, all along, we were
eating buckwheat pancakes every Sunday.

I'll start at midnight, when the registers
reset, checker on break.

I'll slip out with eggs in my pocket.

I'll start when the white-with-pink-blush peaches come in,
when the jam has foamed, when every single pot

in the kitchen crusts in the sink,
when there's not one more clean plate.

When the mail arrives, when both hands hit twelve.
Soon as the kettle boils.

After a license plate with an X in it,
a graveyard, and two fields of cows.

Exactly when a color no one's seen before
dabs straight up in the dawn.

When the bourbon rose's cream petals,
worn as old underwear, loosen

at the hip and drop
to the summer-tired grass.

NOT TOWARDS A REAL, TOWARDS ANOTHER

In order to begin the adventure I must first tell you that there will be
no adventure.
Nobody wanted gingernut. Through discontinuity there will be continuity.
If her eyes are opened or closed, does it matter? Blood leaves. Remnants
of the government. I live here, where else would I want to live? How lost
you looked without your glasses. Cake crumbs were going fast but
the oatmeal
wasn't popular. Melancholy represents a capacity for infinite feeling. What
the hell were you thinking? All night long the sounds of doors and keys.
Dear Peter, buses are always delayed and I'm drunk again. Isolation
occurred
amidst myriad isolations. The moon came in through the slats. Her mates
were touching her with their antennae as if puzzled by such crazy behavior.
Singing: *Yer gonna lose a good thing*. At times a certain feeling hangs
weights upon me, like madstones. Girl in a soft pink hat. Someone
has found the buttons and mice with crystal-studded collars.
The last word on page 129, which is missing, is
. There will be a small death in this poem.
Hello.
Dear sir: I regret to inform you that I did not find you at the bottom of
my soup.
Sad-eyed 1939. We didn't know where we were. Thank goodness we
saw you.
Had to—what was he up to?—laughed outright. One false step and it's
bye-bye Raoul.
The twig caterpillar deceives the moth. Dear Gregory, in the other part
of my dream.
This time he hoped for a chance to see more but did not after all. Not
attached
to any specific *existence*, not attached to life. You beautiful kiddo.
And the blossom beetles bore us bravely, though we were heavy with jam.

NURSEMAID'S ELBOW

A PARTIAL DISLOCATION OF THE ELBOW, CAUSED BY A SUDDEN PULL ON A CHILD'S ARM OR HAND

For K.F.

Named not for the mother, frazzled and rushed,
nor for the toddler who knows just when to flop.

Not for the swinging up from her tantrum,
nor for how swiftly it happens, the soft

chicken-wing pop. Not for the child
silent in ER, unable to lift

her left arm, nor for the X-ray showing
her radius slipped from its usual spot.

Not for the doctor cupping her elbow,
turning her palm back and up. Not for his thumb

finessing the ligament, nor for how
soon she's playing again with her dolls. But

for this: stern servant, hired helpstress, easy
scapegoat—the one who was not even there.

ON WHIDBEY ISLAND

On the day she died, not knowing
        this would be the day,
he coaxed her outside and they worked

around the two tall pines that leaned
        the same way, that stood
near each other like twins. They put

an S-curve of large rounded rocks
        at the base of one tree, looped
the rocks in lessening size as they

rounded the other tree. A rusty length
        of salvaged boat chain
completed the curve, as though to say

something about how the man-made
        was merely part of what
had always been there: the gray rocks

from the nearby beach, the driftwood
        shaped like plowshares
and lightning, turning white among

the new rhododendrons. In the lagoon
        in front of their house,
a foursome of hooded mergansers,

a lone heron backlit in late silver light,
        a kingfisher hovering then
plunging, but too far to confirm if it had

caught anything. Because kingfishers
        keep in pairs, when she
found one dead from having flown into

a window, she knew the other would
        come looking, which it did.
This was not a metaphor for anything,

but simple fact. The fact of water,
    grass, trees, houses, cells, blood.
The fact of a last day's work, then

the start of dying. The fact of what one
    intends, and what happens.
The bird calling and calling and calling.

OTHER WORDS

We stare at the pockmarked sky,
whisper asbestos instead of clouds.

When the plane touches down
we thank Buddy Holly,
not God, Allah, or Goodness.

We say dishrag or ribtaker
instead of homemaker.
Use whiplash and lackluster
instead of breadwinner.

We say numbskull when we mean numbskull,
and blonde when we mean smart; we know
brunette is synonymous with attentive.

Let's have foxtrot instead of foreplay
and vampire bites instead of menstrual cramps.

Still, what can we substitute for childbirth?
Bamboozle? Inferno? Divinity?

There are days when sippy cups
become purgatory and family vacation
suggests space mission.

We try to talk while doing the bills,
but it turns into a mudslide. We try to speak

truthfully, but it becomes a storm watch,
tsunami warning, the dune on the beach
covered with glass.

I don't want to say fishhook
when I mean marriage, or not-tonight
when what I want to say is: I can't explain
my sadness or the night has stolen the sky.

FROM "PASSAGES"

Today I felt unlike myself. I left my apartment, walked up to the closest version of myself I could find.

He was a man in a spire
or scrap of music;

in an Italian peacoat sometimes, sometimes in sweats, toes poking through his shoes.
Carrying a parcel, he bled through his fingers—no, clutched a teacup full of pink paint.

Had the eyes of a child.

PLATO'S BAD HORSE

I wanted Plato's bad horse,
not the good one, set on discourse and decorum.
I wanted the horse that pulls toward
the radiant face of the beloved.

He takes the bit shamelessly:
a great jumble of a beast, thick-necked,
bleary-eyed. He is, we are expressly told,
the mate of insolence and knavery.

The good horse, upright and clean-limbed,
boasts an aquiline nose, a milk-white eye.
He will drench the soul in penitential sweat,
take the teeth out of intemperate desire.

But Plato's bad horse is part scapegoat
and part ox. (I'd seen oxen tremble in unison,
and then, bellies to the earth like improbable
mice, creep forward in a liquid movement

that unseated marble slabs.)
Only after much bit-yanking and plying
of the whip will the sight of the beloved
bring the bad horse to his knees.

*

One off-season, my mother stabled two horses:
they were both bad, and consequently,
drew the phantom chariot of their desires
evenly over the field, the Indian paintbrush,

the half-rusted fern announcing the stone wall
that ran beside the woods. She herself had become
misshapen with desire: she wanted to keep living,
like the roans—

She found delicate work for the fingers
along their parsed necks, little stopping places,
elaborate as the fretwork of a flute,
that maintained in her the ability to dwell...

And this is how my mother left me, her hands
offering solace to those difficult beasts
whose existence slipped my mind even before
they were dispatched to parts unknown.

My memories have become too blurred
to be of use, like horses that cannot be ridden.
Like my mother's roans pulling in tandem
to join the halves of what I still don't know.

POETRY

Nobody at any rate reads it much. Your
lay
citizenry have other forms of fun.

Still, who would wish to live in a culture
of which future anthropologists would say
Oddly, they had none?

PROCESSIONAL

The sky unfurls
its monotone gray light
to a smattering
of rain and gold leaves.
A wren sings
the same three notes
as yesterday
when clouds
were peach-colored
roses pinned
to the mountain's
black lapel.

RECEDING UNIVERSE RAG

I'm one bone away from a very bright man—
One beep from the solar age.
One glass of milk from a collar bone—
One microwave from the beep.

One drop away from a glass of milk—
One floor from the microwave.
One straw away from the sucking drop—
One ocean from the floor.

One cent away from a box of straws—
One league from oceaning.
One job away from an honest cent—
One nation from a league.

One call away from a menial job—
One state from national.
One beck away from a beck and call—
One being from a state.

One song away from being Beck—
One just from being me.
One warble from a sing-along—
One criminal from the just.

One cat away from warblerless—
One act from criminal.
One pop-rock from a fraidy-cat—
One method from an act.

ROUND EARTH'S CORNER

Take operation's shimmy all the way back,
spot where my hand on the fridge handle un-
hands whole networks: PG&E pumping

its box-car'd, coal-jumped generators,
the hectic electric passing its bright idea
to last week's Buddha Delight back there,

gone bad. I hold the door open till the hum
starts. Cold seeps from the chamber. A shiver
now at the neck. Then closed, then the sidling

miles of cable keeping me connected, the metals
dug, welded, smelted from cooling cores,
bauxite and ore, beat to un-airy thinness,

underground passages, new flanged steel.
All that's rolled, snipped, fitted, piped
to reach my unit, me, a paying customer,

heart thumping steady, my veins branched
in need of these rivets, bolts, coils, rubber
tubes and tape. The sum trained to wipe neat

in a blink if dinner drips down the white
laminate door when the container spills. Dear
Power service, if I am standing before my coffin-

sized hole of near-freezing to take from, tell me I am
the thought you think, one synapse among the many
reuptakes, sitting down for its huge plate of food.

SAUDADE

"THE DESIRE TO BE AFAR"

A boy, I moved from coast to coast,
Learning that five years was as long
As a home in any state could last:
To stay in one place for good was wrong.

The Portuguese explorers knew
This hunger—the urge that makes a man
Seek another world. The blue
That lined their west pulled the sun

Beyond their shores. The sailors wondered
Where the sun kept going. What country
Could call down such fire like a bird
To a branch, fusing sky and sea?

A man, I feared the fog and rain
Of Seattle would seal me in their gauze.
So I joined the poster navy: men
Turned gold by the sun, like all those

Who search for home in the horizon.
Five years I crossed the Atlantic
Until my own land had grown foreign:
Strange enough to call me back.

SEA CREATURES OF THE DEEP

O sockeye O rock sole O starry flounder
O red Irish lord O spiny lumpsucker

Dear threespine stickleback, sweet broken-back shrimp—
hear the dreadful voices from the balcony. You're the blind

taking the bull by the horns. You're snow on a stick,
a stuck jukebox, a ribbon-swamped trike. O gum boot,

O lemon peel nudibranch—do not fear the leafy hornmouth;
dogwinkle and moon snail walk the floor and burn their bridges.

Lonely whitecap limpet, days are not true. You stand on one foot,
and we brush past. To live a life is not to walk across a field.

Pity the ghost shrimp, heart on his sleeve, or the glassy sea squirt,
run through with tears. O to have gathered no moss, to know a clam's

muddy joy. You shut with a snap, you blur with silt, you poke
among barnacles. A bunch of one-trick ponies, even brave wolf eel.

Cornered, the plainfin midshipman sings when afraid.
They say it fears only the elusive cloud sponge.

SEWARD PARK

for Larry Knappert, now past tense

Our situation is
Lake Washington in dusk,
silver as an ironing board cover.
Some five ducks

troubled by his
saying if there is a God I've got
some questions for the motherfucker
mutter something and swim off.

Seattle, Mercer Island, these insects,
all this crinkly rigmarole
slips into the dimming envelope.

My friend Aprils taught me to say
motherfucker in a way
that carries with it some respect.

SO LONG MOON SNAIL

pulled,
up, lulling,
from the cold canal by the naughty
boys of Vaughn in their dory.
I only offered you my open

palm—
sweet eons
of saffron sea grass, falling tides, whorled
worm shells and starfish curled
awkwardly to escape the sun's new

heat
now beating
down unbearably on us. I won't
forget, flat-footed one,
traveling all the way from Triassic

mud,
how you touched
me. You took my warmth and gave it back.
Expanding, you relaxed
and I forgot your skill at plying

bi-
valves riding
the silt drift. Such persuasive presence.
Not even the caress
of your sandpaper rasp reminded

me.
Ecstasies
of the Native Little Neck! Before
she knows you've even bored
a beveled hole, you're there, inside her

shell.
She's all filled
with you and then she's gone. Only the grace
of the bad boys who'd first placed
us together saved me. They tossed you over

board,
mottled Lord
of mollusks, you sank away, leaving me
to ponder your gentle
willingness to wait for whomever

might.

THE ANGELS

are not like the saints.

They do not discriminate
but come to everyone.

Their eyes burn green fire
but their kisses are icy.

They can play rough when we get caught
in the heavy crosswinds that swirl about their wings.

They are not above artifice
and sometimes appear in disguise:

a mask of smeared lipstick, gypsy
bangles, or an old man's coat.

Now and again they carelessly give us gifts:
an unexpected hobbyhorse, a day's free babysitting,

a poke in the eye with a stick,
or sudden slant of light on water.

And we are grateful, once we figure out how
to move within their state of complex blessings.

They work within great wheels and circles,
turning light to dark and back again.

They do not obey the laws of gravity
but laugh a lot and arise at will

to hover like vast hummingbirds
when we require attention.

What they want of us is the mysterious secret
we unravel and reweave

down to dark and back again.

THE ROBOT SCIENTIST'S DAUGHTER [MEDICAL WONDER]

was a bit confused. She started down a road
to medical wonder, sat under the machine's lights,
but then tiptoed off on a paper trail,
looking for an island of cranes. She made a thousand
wishes, still she shed a blue glow
and everyone said *how sickly*. Her nails
made of plastic and paper maché, her heart's
thump-thump three times fast. Her one kidney
curled inside her ribs, her blood trying to escape.
Father she screamed but he couldn't save her.

The robot scientist's daughter knew
what she had to do. With her own two hands
she built a new body, one that worked better
this time, silver and shiny and smooth
as mirrored glass. After all she'd been trained,
it was no less than was expected. She crawled inside
and adjusted the fit. This time, there will be no
stopping her. The curves are all impenetrable
and the precision of each drum-kit-beat keeps her in line.
She's a soldier, a savior, a ship to bear prisoners into space.

THINKING UP A NEW POWER

Unlike oil, the wind is always there, sometimes.
— Frank Murkowski, former governor of Alaska

Sometimes there and others
there. Again it slides through, moves
over swaying stalks of kelp
or Anchorage with ease and all ways
sounding the same in Arabic

as English, Simoom
and Chinook. Clear monument
of moments gathered, it's here
when on its way: red flags flare,
headlines flip in the street,

and every far peak
blurs while buoyant seeds
float its democratic shoulders.
Birds know how to cup
its slight adjustments. Could its breath

be the way we breathe,
shifting, failing and strong? It is
our only state, offering
from the start an ocean depth
and the slightest nod.

VAGRANTS & ACCIDENTALS

Above the house, helicopters have been circling
all morning: rattling
the fuchsia bushes, alarming the hummingbirds.

Whose world is this anyway, chop-chop?
My neighbor winces at the sky, unnerved,
trying to read the pollen count.

In my view, that's the pure purpose trivets serve,
patterning dust,
though my view has been narrowing

since time began. Look: past the vanishing point
to the right of the fire station,
a Steller's Jay pokes at my plump cufflinks.

I'm dressing for a wedding or waiting
for redress. Nor is a Steller's Jay
native to my wardrobe—must have been caught

in a freak summer storm.
Your letters task
the listlessness which overcomes me

while the helicopters hover ever louder
overhead. Will they catch the truant fugitive?
Is the freeway traffic wriggling free?

I keep my eye
on that piece of atmosphere,
that wormhole of Pacific

jet stream pouring through my window
some mornings emptier than others,
ferociously calm, spiked with the long notes

of a painted redstart. There's nothing not
trivial about a crossroads. Wherever you are,
send word.

WEARING A BABYBJÖRN

Into a liquor store with your five-month-old
facing the thirsty horde of George C. Scotts
and Betty Fords, like a chubby, ruddy shield.

The undead stare, as they should: you are sad,
a young man with a soft sacrifice strapped to
his chest, and you are searching for anything

that's forty proof. Speaking of which—you've
forgotten your identification, which you realize
as you pull a bottle of bourbon off the top shelf

—but you have a baby for god's sake. Isn't that
proof enough of your manhood? You squeeze
the expensive vessel by its red, waxy neck, and

approach a register, getting in line behind Liz
Taylor and Richard Burton who are reloading.
Your son makes prehistoric sounds at a window

and it's hard to say who is more of a man—you,
George C., or the woman who is carrying nothing,
pushing a stroller past the store without stopping.

WEST COAST

Mike's up from Noe Valley one Friday
and we go out to The Copper Gate
in Ballard with his in-laws, for the pickled
herring and strange Danish cheeses.
Decorating the restaurant bathroom
hang light boxes displaying nude
women posing in black-and-white,
and men who are dressed like women.
This used to be a sailor's bar, and what
remains is this form of their loneliness,
and it becomes mine for a few hours,
reminding my body of its lusts
for close skin and how different from light
skin is, more like glass, or the breathing
of a horse in a dark, sodden field.
We split off from the group to ramble
the provincial streets, wander bookstores
in and out, bars, a burger stand.
Kansas is a cold dessert, I say.
No, Kansas is a tongue depressor, he says.
You can't speak freely. The aquavit
we drink is clear as the rust of stars,
and my mind is shaped like a prow,
all black wood and forward riding.
When we return to The Copper Gate,
the only light remaining is above the grill,
a thin tube like a line in a play,
a minimalist play, said over and over.
The cook has gone home. The waiter,
with her hair back-combed may be
asleep beside her burly new love
under a white comforter, because
the aquavit she served us, flavored
like rye bread, allows me to think so.
We're still up, walking the streets,
looking for ketchup for the fries
Mike has discovered in his jacket,
and we are trying to remember which kid
it was at the pool hall back in Topeka
who bragged he could bend his body

and kiss his own penis, and showed us
I think in the alley, but Mike says no,
not the kid who could pop out his eye
made of glass, and let you handle it
for a dollar, but Cliff, who knocked
Mike down after a basketball game,
for winning, and he never showed us.
Our high-minded speculation fades
as we try to find the car, remembering
only that it faced the ship locks,
and when we find it we eat the fries
cold, and let the paper bag be taken
by the wind along the water, and settle
onto its currents, among the rustling gulls.

WHAT I WILL TELL THE ALIENS

I will tell them about our clapping,
our odometers, and our skillets.

I will take them to a place of fierce
lightning, to a place of tombstones

and of gridlock, and I will tell them
of geckos, of ecstatic moments,

all about our tchotchkes, our temples,
our granite-countered kitchens.

Give me an alien and I will give it
a story of unfathomable odds,

of erections and looting. Show me
an alien and I will show it the sorrows

of the centuries, all wrapped up
in a kerchief, all wrapped up

in a grandmother's black wool coat.
Bring me an alien right now,

and I will show it the misery
of stilettos, of pounding out

tortillas and gyros. Please—
send me an alien, and I will give it

a bloody nose, and then I will show it a great
humanitarian gesture, 10,000 tents

when 600,000 are needed. Let me
talk to these aliens about shoe-shiners

and rapture, of holidays and faxes;
let me pray with the aliens for the ice

to stop melting, for the growths to stop
growing, for a gleam to remain on our lips
long after the last greasy French fry is gone.

WHAT THE SEA TAKES

One day's catch recorded in the log: forty sockeye, fifteen chums, seven cohos, a white king. A receipt book, yellow pages thick as an accordion. A plastic Joy soap bottle, one tennis shoe, left, tongue swollen. *What we keep, what we toss*. The day I dropped the fish pick overboard, watched it sink out of sight; next set, fetched up by the net. The night the storm petrel skittered down on deck, rode with us across the Gulf, then flew. *What the sea takes, gives back*. The fisherman gone overboard found the next morning, boat adrift, tangled in his net.

WITHOUT A WORD

At dawn today a coyote (say it right:
two syllables, accent on the first)
no doubt at the conclusion of his night
of delving into rabbit burrows burst
from tangled undergrowth, but when he heard
me tramping down the path he stopped and gazed
at me as if he sought the coyote word
to make me out as food or foe. He raised
his nose to catch my scent, more evidence
to help him place me in his lexicon.
But I was not in any important sense
to him a predator or prey, and on
two legs without potential as a mate.
If coyotes shrug away an unconcern
he did, and took up his unhurried gait.
A hundred yards away I saw him turn
his head to give a last, dismissive look,
then glide without a sound the way he came,
begrudging me the little time he took
to find that I was nothing he need name.

WORDS IN THE KEY OF C

You hesitate at it.
The shape of a wedge,

door stop or stop at the door;
cunctation—akin to he wavers.

You are cunning
and present

for the moments
before.

Culmination:
a thick tongue through it.

The accumulation
dense as cumulus clouds

gathered above
that hold their moisture in

for the final show.
I am the cup. Full,

held at your lips,
and readied for communion,

to celebrate the piece of me
we do not name aloud.

YOU MIGHT CONSIDER

how my long life of losing men
could create a new international sport.

Men lost in the desert, men missing
in action from doorways and all-night diners;

men making the most of fire
escapes, service stairs, the emergency aisle

of airplanes like *United*. Men
parasailing after spaceship encounters.

I am accomplished in the world
of the see-you-later wave

as his pickup truck disappears
traveling to the next espresso stand.

Something in the curve of my collar,
the blue of my blouse sets them running.

They know they are in the hands of a master.
But when the coffee's on, the pumpernickel

toasted just right, I have to let them know;

I'm actually ready for them to go.

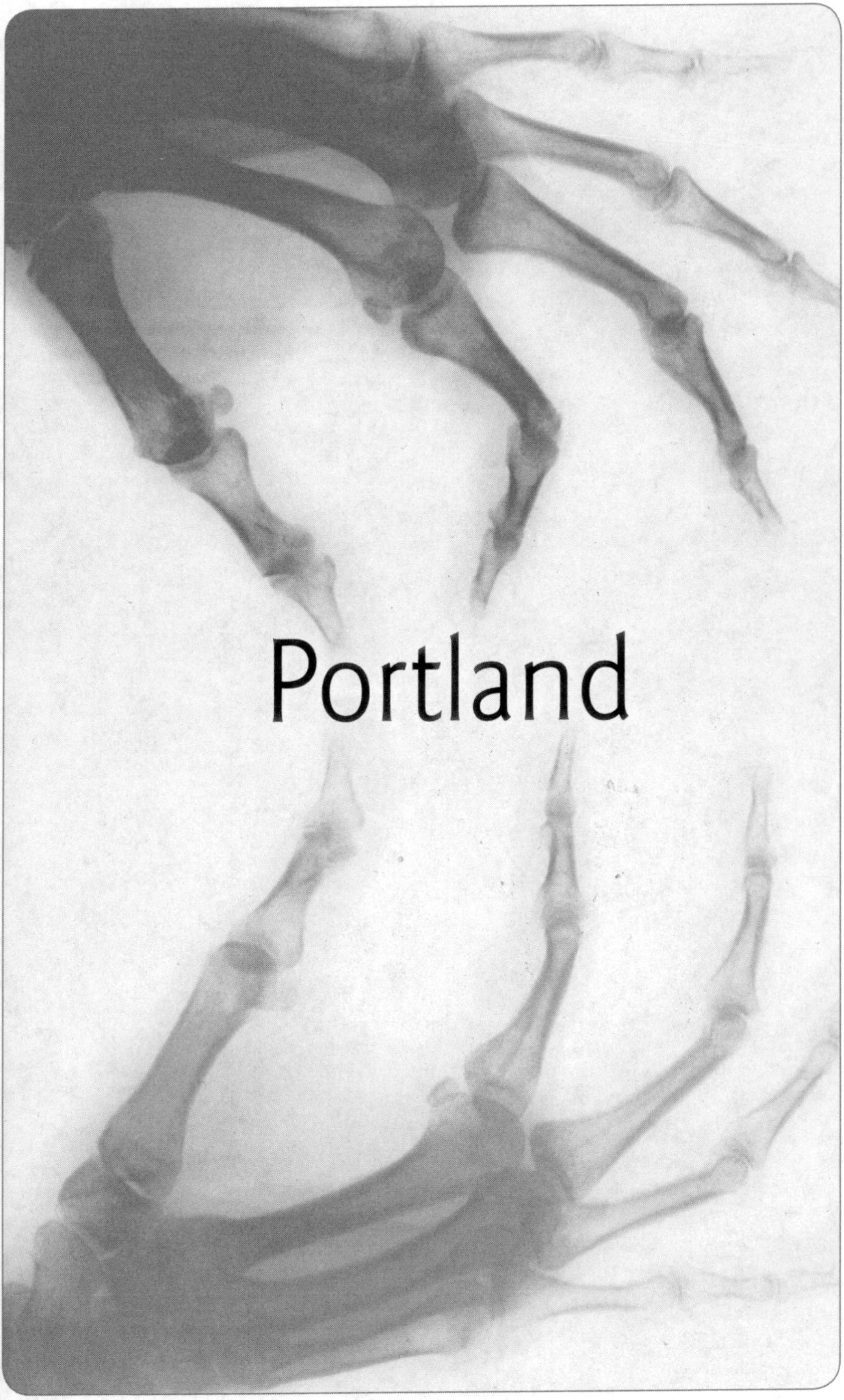

Portland

POEMS FROM PORTLAND, OREGON

We put together a selection of Portland poets. Some of them don't live here, but they belong to us. Some of them live close by—Eugene, Corvallis, Monmouth—we share the Willamette Valley. They're ours.

Sometimes they refer to poets of any given region as a tribe. It kind of bugs me. I'm not sure why. When people refer to the tribe of poets, I think of Liam Neeson in *Rob Roy*, with men in kilts roaming the Scottish Highlands. I fear we lack the wardrobe to really be called tribal.

The Cosmic Baseball Association is an online fantasy baseball team, made up of poets, philosophers, and artists. Imagining the poets of Portland as a baseball team seems a little more appropriate. For example:

> Walt Curtis thinks playing baseball is a super fantastic terrific idea and is flirting with the umpire, but really just wants to make sure no one gets hurt. Mary Syzbist is pitching fastballs, and Paulann's bat just made contact. Biespiel's running towards the fence.
>
> Jesse reminds us how incredibly cool we all are, even when we feel like total doofuses in the outfield. Carl and Crystal were radiant and rapt while we explained the rules to them, but they've been running around the backstop and tripping the catcher all afternoon.

Of course the metaphor gets forced at a certain point. The poets of this region are no more a baseball team than we are an ancient tribe. No, wait—we are. We're a tribe, a baseball team, we're an organized, inept crime syndicate, we're transparently ambitious used car salesmen, we're an off-key, melodic high school choir. We're an extended family with relatives that inspire, confuse, frustrate us—but we always invite them home for Thanksgiving because it wouldn't be a celebration without them.

We're in collusion and opposition. We meant to come to your reading but couldn't get the baby to sleep, had to prepare for class tomorrow, had to mow the lawn—but could you please just take a moment to read this poem we wrote yesterday? We think it's really good—does the ending seem forced? We came to your reading and your work was so amazing we decided there was no point in trying to write another poem ever again. You were just that brilliant and we secretly started wishing you'd leave town—no, not really. We were proud to live in the same town with you—to know we might see you writing at a table in our neighborhood coffee shop, we might run into you at Powell's—and we went home and stayed up all night. We stole all your metaphors and witty asides, and made them ours. We knew you wouldn't mind.

I don't know if Portland poets write with their landscape in mind. Some of them can't escape it, and some of them are confounded by other things.

So sure, it's Oregon, go ahead—mention the rain and the Doug Firs and the fish and the rivers that run through it all. Some of us can't help but notice these things. Thank you for noticing them in a way that reminds us why we can't take them for granted, that reminds us why Tom McCall called this Eden.

But also remember—this is Stumptown. A long time ago people came here and cut down all the trees, so they could build some houses, stick around awhile.

So if you don't know if a steelhead is a salmon or a trout, and you keep forgetting what deciduous means, consider the names of some of our reading series: Loggernaut, If Not For Kidnap, Spare Room, Mountain Writers, Bad Blood. Consider the names of some of the poems found here: *Dismantling. Enlightment. Accidents of Trees. Distant Friends. Exile Off Foster.*

The poets of Portland are waiting for you.

—*Susan Denning*

A MAN WHO WAS AFRAID OF LANGUAGE

The houses, the trees, and the dust had become
Sentences having nothing to do with themselves.
He seldom left his apartment now, the only refuge

He could endure, the dank spaces
And dim lights, the phone and radio unplugged.
Even printed works went on shifting

And crossing while stray phrases, echoes of phrases
Took up the burden. He tried to think
Of the same thing again and again.

He closed the blinds, but the boys still came
With their taunts and jokes and vulgar songs.
Sunlight slanted into their eyes.

A woman in blue made ambiguous gestures.

ACCIDENTS OF TREES

In columns and rows
they grew sideways for spite
or confusion, elbowed
for light.

In these tidy rows the whippoorwills
disorient and cannot rest.

The dust boiled as they fell
into square bright pools of field.

The wild trees, not far away,
stood on tiptoe. The new ones
in delicate tangles of root
where the nurses once fed them,
and old survivors licked black
where they'd opened their skirts.

Toward the straight forest
long throats leaned forward
shushing the birds.

ANNUNCIATION: EVE TO AVE

The wings behind the man I never saw.
But often, afterward, I dreamed his lips,
Remembered the slight angle of his hips,
His feet among the tulips and the straw.

I liked the way his voice deepened as he called.
As for the words, I liked the showmanship
With which he spoke them. Behind him, distant ships
Went still; the water was smooth as his jaw—

And when I learned that he was not a man—
Bullwhip, horsewhip, unzip, I could have crawled
Through thorn and bee, the thick of hive, rosehip,
Courtship, lordship, gossip and lavender.
(But I was quiet, quiet
As eagerness—that astonished, dutiful fall.)

APPETITE

Pale gold and crumbling with crust
mottled dark, almost bronze,
pieces of honeycomb lie on a plate.
Flecked with the pale paper
of hive, their hexagonal cells
leak into the deepening pool
of amber. On your lips,
against palate, tooth and tongue,
the viscous sugar squeezes
from its chambers, sears sweetness
into your throat until you chew
pulp and wax from a blue city
of bees. Between your teeth
is the blown flower and the flower's
seed. Passport pages stamped
and turning. Death's officious hum.
Both the candle and its anther
of flame. Your own yellow hunger.
Never say you can't take
this world into your mouth.

AVULSION

And though I grieved, my time in hell
was sure and short. Those gaseous veins
of gorgeous mineral states told me more
than I could know on the sedgy plains of earth.

There was no voice like yours
in hell. The saxophones were verdigris
and cold. There was no voice at all,
not yours, and not my own.

I cannot say whose empty house it was
that burned throughout the wrinkled night.
I can tell you that morning brought intelligent
blue light not seen by anyone on earth.

I don't remember much—just this:
the lid was screwed on tight
and no one cared if heaven fell
to earth or gathered us in light.

BETWEEN BRANCHES AND WIND

Escucha, sólo escucha el estruendo del oleaje, mientras el mirlo clama entre las ramas y el viento.
—Jaime Luís Huenún

leapt, this time, into a space that had been
 assembling, as had we, gathering
in particles and
   in the dark, a space
against

which we might come
            and, bracketed
 by raw limbs
above us,
allied in a null state, here
 in movement and in a temp-

orary rise
  beyond will,
expedience, charge,
  let enter us what was carried on
 the air: the least
syllable, its least counterpart.

after-
image of a wing that in lifting
  also masks
its voice. this view is a
void,
a sway or
its echo, and all of it a
   relative still-
ness carved, we say,
for us, the long

tail
of a crash, a line of
decay, if unbroken,
bursting at the end into
  glitter,
running in, as a condition,
as motor and
  as fuel for
wind,
the stunter of the branch under
which we keep
a safe
distance—
and from each

other:
sound of a making
and slower
unmaking, breaking, within
  and beneath, as we
know, the same
wheel.

BLOODLINE

The moon is wet nurse
to roses. She suckles
each soft-mouthed poppy.

Blame her for menses.
Rail at her for the craving
to binge and purge.

Please her when you choose
to delay the day for planting,
biding your time
until night has fattened
her silver torso. Praise her
when the fleck of seed
poked down into damp dark
takes hold and swells.

Any girl-child is always
her offspring.

Upbraid her for your daughter's
sass and door-slams,
that hot hurry to be what most
differs from you.

Long ago, the moon decided
on a pathway against the route
stars take. No one else
would dare to walk
the black sky backward.

BLOOM AND DECAY

1

These twisted ivy patches are not a tale of pursuit, and any unraveling
That binds us—rituals of envy, outlived slurs, old burns—
Has us stomaching odd moods that we get sick over but still obey.
If you silence the sky, my love, I'll close the boulevard down.
If you run hard in sleet and wind, then walk out of your life,
I'll stop at last in this city and die.

2

All evening now this city has been closer at hand and shinier—
The understory leaving us inseparable and maddened—
While the flinty candlelights in the window thin and canter,
Bloom and decay, and without question
Our eyes have opened to blackness and what is left unsaid:
This passage of delight is our sorrow and our bed.

BORING

I was going to say something, but it was boring.
It's more interesting if you wonder what it was.
Birds are boring, unless they're indoors.
Paper is a little less boring when it's folded into animals.
I bought a plant and its pot was terra cotta,
which is boring, so I painted it. This made the plant
look boring, so I painted it too—you know the rest.
My old car was rusted in spots, so I added a stripe.
Is it excited that racing days lie ahead? Probably not.
My boss is boring, so when he talks
I imagine a polar bear behind him.
Steve Martin wished for a month-long orgasm,
but that would get boring after a week or so.
You should think of what you find boring.
This thing right here is boring, you were just thinking,
which is wonderful—it's all part of the experience.
Sandwiches bore me to sleep. Sleep is never boring.
Computers are deathly boring, so I keep thinking
of painting over mine's plastic beige with a woodland scene
in spastic kid colors, but I haven't found the time.
I love everything very poorly.

COUNTRY MUSIC

When the dark finds us
full-throated, singing
of bright mother & river-dead men,
& our dim Audrey lost to another,
let the words bless us
somehow, a ceiling of fire
above our heads—
& let The Caller huddle near
with his ether strings, his beautiful
wounds, his waves of grass
Let us hang in the night until this passes.

DISMANTLING

Call Joel (eves) 623-9765

Smack in the public eye
at Ninth and Van Buren, tearing down
an old house—
"Not demolition, dismantling!" says Joel. Slowly
we make the house disappear.
It takes a few months.
We do this for a living.
Our sign says:
USED LUMBER FOR SALE.
Neat stacks of it on the front lawn
around a dormant forsythia—
shiplap and siding, and over here
we have two-by…
That pile is already sold.

We also have toilets, sinks, remarkable
savings on bent nails,
French doors, free kindling
and more. Lots more.

…

With the roof off
a house looks more like a cathedral,
rafters outlined against the sky.
A pair of ragged priests,
we celebrate
nothing stick by stick. We are making the shape of
nothing,
creating
an absence.

And when we have finished,
what will there be at Ninth and Van Buren?
A square of bare earth
where a house was.
Sidewalk. Foundation. Concrete stoop.
Two steps up
and you're there.

DISTANT FRIENDS

That year we both lost fathers, even though,
natural aristocrat, you didn't say so
and I spoke of nothing else. For me

the world was like a country road running
between field burns gone out of control, turning
the air acrid and opaque with smoke,

and what I mourned—lost comfort or stove-in
safety, haven, or, more simply, the loving—
I could not say then. Now, years later,

I wonder at you, seeming so able
outwardly, but underneath like a small bull
terrier wrestling with an intruder

or bone. It still seems a kind of wisdom
to me looking back: such delicate tact or calm,
practiced loss dexterously plowed under.

DON'T ASK, DON'T TELL

It's all gray at the bridge toll backup. It's winter,
it's always winter here, and raining hard,
when it's your turn to drive.

Your new rideshare companion curls up like a cat
in the heated leather seat beside you. Asian,
though French you guess from her purr.

She's twenty, maybe twenty-four. You found her
on Craigslist. You know nothing about her
and of course she knows nothing of you.

She's comfortable enough in your escort—she's
slowly nodding off—but when you reach down
for the stick, she grips the leather strap of her

black workbag a little harder, as if rendered
by an early morning dream that has returned
and taken hold.

You turn up the heat and she breathes uneasily,
shifts in her seat. Though when her flushed
cheek turns, she smiles like daybreak, breath

tinctured with sage, raspberry, warm Belgian
chocolate—It doesn't matter that you could be her
father, or her mother. It doesn't matter if you are a

woman, or a man. The distance between you is con-
founding—you don't know if you can trust yourself
with the truth.

DRAWING LESSON

A step toward loss, no colors.
The glass, the leaves, the branches—all gray.

These are your words, your few words. It's a diminishment,
a necessary lesson you try

to view as a choice, a humble garden,
an arrangement of shades. The butterfly of pleasure

now a moth, an accurate line,
a plane possessing its proper shade.

You look and look, your hand disobeys,
but sometimes the pencil gets it right.

What you need to learn: To get by with less,
to represent in a new way. Represent, as if to catch

the present by evaporating into it. I was here,
say the strokes of graphite.

Your tools are simple
so you will not be distracted

by anything but the stick that is set before you—
the stick and its bent, beautiful shadow.

EFFECT

a riddle says x but means x + 1
this is why hands can't
make what they're made of

there's no affliction minister wrapped
in lab-coat white
crawling scuff-kneed and slow
across the linoleum
to ration doubt and be
finally *about* something

here in the nursery
in the laboratory—learning
songs in capillary time

ENLIGHTENMENT

DETROIT, MI

She is merging onto the Edsel Ford Freeway
in a car no longer made,

in a city that no longer makes it,
talking on her cellular phone, slouched to the left,

fingernails purple & red & caging the wheel,
head cocked & foot heavy.

In pursuit of a race car,
she has bought a roll of black duct tape,

has rolled three racing stripes
down the sedan's hood

as if she has been whispering with Buddha
& he said, Sister, relinquish your resistance,

your discomfort, forsake your ego.
Which she has done,

which is what it means to want
but not have

in a city stacked with desire,
to know that desire is our most ruinous trait,

the moment in the morning
when you decide to be unsatisfied & unhappy.

Our want is just one of many in a line of wants
& the line of wants is ancillary to the line of needs.

People close to you are hungry
& you have ignored it.

People close to you have lost their jobs.
Today somebody's mother has died.

Today somebody's child has been murdered.
Today some body lost sight.

& your Lumina runs.
Your Lumina runs well; Luminosity,

woman: No one is coming to save you.
There is nothing from which to be saved.

ERIC CHAVEZ IN PORTLAND

How fortunate life lies, Eric, my never-ending
birth tonight in Portland, you on rehab
with the Sacramento Rivercats,
I a mere nine rows up!

I can see the contours of your face, your brow even,
the perfect Zen in your crouch. Your precise
over-the-shoulder release. The fundamental straightness
of your back. Is that a little belly even?

Every move, every pitch, every waking
high thrust of my spirit simply yards away,
at third, all my lost dreams realized tonight

in your paced extension, gentle lean
slow gait, nervous twitch, gracious act
your glove, my heart.

EUROPE. MEMORY. SQUID PARTS. GRACE.

Whether the squid's ear resembles the diaphanous soul in ascent
or an aerial shot of Cuba,
the macabre happens and happens

Rising like a prayer from my daughter, Svetlana,
remarkable for the grace with which she moved through the insipid
stations of her teens

Educing the woman out of the girl
like scampi brought upriver by cruise ships
and served at the noisy Quinceañeras of East Los Angeles

Kind of detached from reality as evening flickers
and blogs by American males rhizomically expand in the blogspace
and Zeus hauls memory's daughter across the ocean

To an island of prosperous rental property owners
busy remembering Cuba
where Internet cafes are like churches

And churches are like monsters
once believed in and dreaded across pre-Christian Europe
now placed wistfully inside the atriums of the forgotten

as equivocal as fog, as curtains, as darkness, as closed doors.

EXILE OFF FOSTER

I worked past the first winter
to yesterday, when someone was stabbed
to death on the street behind me,
the first day of spring. Pistols were drawn
outside my back window, a police sniper
crouched on my neighbor's roof.
We gathered at the end of the block
for the first time, the neighbors,
like a poor man's United Nations,
smelling of beets, cocaine, and body odor:
the crack dealer, the laborer, the bartender,
the ice cream man. On this side
of the city that's yet to be in fashion,
we share two things—a history
of before here and a feeling for having settled.
In a city of trees, there are few here,
yet an abundance of birds—crows, robins,
scrub jays, finches, and hawks—that too
have resigned. They rest where we have given up,
eat from the overgrown lots.
I came here out of circumstance
and am now surrounded by organ meat,
diesel fuel, rusted radiators, dandelions,
overgrown rhododendrons covered
with dead blooms, pit bulls,
and babushka-wearing yentas
who roll their metal carts full of dinged boxes.
Soon a few desperate farmers
will put out what they've grown
on the rain-soaked dirt and gravel.
Anything to survive. Bring in some money
and vitamins. I had a family
of raccoons living in my eaves last summer.
At night, they would stare at me
from the corner of my roof.
I suppose the lesson I was meant to learn

was that anyone can make a home
out of anything, so long as you're comfortable
with your lot. But the rest of us
don't seem comfortable. I toss and turn
at night. Everyone fidgets with their fingers.
And even though these are still
somewhat my people, from the Ukraine,
from Staten Island, from the far Pacific,
and from what was once all of Mexico,
something doesn't translate. Not even
my grandmother wore a babushka
and her collapsible shopping cart
was left behind years ago, cigarettes
soon after. I've hung on
to caraway seeds, sticky white rice,
the talisman that hangs next to my front door,
and a blind faith in hard work.
But I'm no longer sure that it's enough
to build a community with.
For all the interest that we might have
in each other, the only dialogue is exchanged
with loose change. Chessboards
and park benches have disappeared.
My name is never called,
my shoulder is never tapped.
And yesterday, as quickly as the man died
on the asphalt, near silence has returned.
The crow's squawk and the cars' bass
remain the only conversation.
On Sunday mornings, the bells from the church
up the road ring, but I've yet to hear
a single lullaby sung. This is a place
where even the ugly have a hard time
falling in love and only the lucky
can recognize beauty. But we're trying.
For God's sake I know that I am,
harder than I've ever done so before.
Here, the one who walked elsewhere runs.
The one who ran now flies.
The one who flew becomes holy.

And no matter who I am now
and no matter what I have done
to have a block of whores closer to me
than a good cup of black coffee.
No matter that my hands are full of slivers
and my feet are finally beginning to crack.
No matter. I want to be holy.

FIRST ICE

We wake up as the darkness begins
giving way, first to an indigo

glow like laundry bluing,
phosphorescent and implausibly dense.

Shades of trees appear, then trees,
then a dreamy, scintillant

stillness unfurls as light, as landscape
under a spell. A fat sleekness

blisters and thickens the porch; in the pasture
grass blades bow down in glass sleeves.

The woods are themselves and not
themselves in their subtle glister,

the way a truly glamorous woman,
my grandmother used to say (charm bracelets rustling),

conceals every seam and trace
of her artifice, leaving pure effect.

Inside, a chef on TV makes aspic
while we wait for the forecast.

One strives for the clearest, thinnest
gel, he is saying; one wants to illuminate

one's terrine, not to thicken it!
And as he spreads his glaze, I see the soul

rise from its loaf and lay its glossy
immaterial bliss across that surface of meat &

salt with its scallion fleur-de-lis,
making it marvelous.

As the world is, today—as it was
in the beginning, that last instant

water, matter and light were one,
each distinct, not yet separate.

HEAVEN DESCRIBED

(IN THE LANGUAGE OF VISITOR'S PAMPHLETS COLLECTED FROM THE GREYHOUND BUS STATION IN PASCO, WASHINGTON)

Hand-picked, you will enter   past
hulks of long-silenced   waterfalls

Through immaculate   life-sized darkness
new varieties of lilac   and now

Can browse   beyond the Milky Way's
cool husks   shimmer

And hang   among the whispers
your offering   pure

Among   hand-picked
positive attitudes   forms

We will provide   the taste
the fruit   wildly holds

HOME, BUT HOME

The war at the bar
was on mute.
You should have heard
the songs the
jukebox played.
"It's a Family Affair."
What I can say
about the war is
I have been working
to make imaginary
enemies visionary.
You know the voices
crowding down,
I let them say what
they say. I
almost apologize.

I AM PREGNANT WITH MY MOTHER'S DEATH

I grow great with her decline. When shall I be delivered?
I'll be there tomorrow, I say on the phone. She's amazed
when I arrive. *Have you met my aide?* she asks politely,
the same kind aide she's had for months.

She remembers to worry, *Do you need more blankets?*
Her radio loud in the airless house, the oxygen machine
humming and spitting as she curls on a waterproof pad.
Oooh, she moans in her sleep, *Ooh, I'm sorry. Ooooh*

thank you. I love you. I'm sorry. I love you. Ooooh.
I wake her. A gradual smile blooms. *I'm embarrassed*
she laughs, *to be such a bag of bones*. Her shrunken
skeleton kicks at my heart and inside my belly.

I'm the luckiest woman in the world, she tells me again,
I'm the luckiest woman in the world. Or else she says,
I'm the loveliest woman in the world, and doesn't notice
any difference. She touches my cheek.

This is something new in our shared lives, how she turns
so gentle. I labor hard with her. Forgiveness loosens
my stubborn bones. I am swollen with her love for me.
When shall I be delivered?

ICELANDIC CHURCH

A blind horse stands amid ash
inches from a long fall to sea.
Mostly bone, pared down to necessity,
muzzling black rock for a taste
of the grass nearby, where all day, sated,
I have watched him.

Night again is taking me like a song.
Like God, says the farmer
who is also a priest
who sleeps in the barn
during my stay.

Alive at the center of bundled hay,
the farmer and his bliss.
I cannot quite taste the mountain
behind the mountain.
And so alive in the hesitant harvest,
an unsteady cliff and its drownings.
Alive in the silent machines left rusted
and the steeple newly painted
and the horse cut from the horizon,
silhouetted in light.

IN MY ALTERNATE LIFE

In my alternate life
I visit *Untitled, 1949* every Sunday afternoon,
and sometimes it hangs in a kitchen
and sometimes in a tea room in Abergavenny in Wales.
In my alternate life I'm Chinese or Brazilian.
I'm walking a beach scattered with slate, it being Cornwall.
Hills, hedgerows, stoats, and a prairie of flowers,
and my mother sleeps in a hammock
and my father sketches her into a book.
I order at the lunch counter
that was *Nighthawks* the night before.
I sit on the stool opposite the coffee urns.
My old back feels sturdy as it did when I was eight,
sun lights the ochre wall like terracotta jazz,
nobody bothers me, the cup never drained.
How have I forgotten the name of this piazza,
Florence, the one with Dante
swirling his stone cloak? Walk three blocks any way
and I'll be lost.
Sometimes swans, sometimes vultures.
Air sings oxygen like after lightning.
Boredom slides like a dime under a cushion.
It perches like a pigeon on my head.
And if I want to talk with someone,
there he is—young or old, American or dead or not—
there she is. Stars anytime.
Imagination scares me less.
People are tolerant and the world is just.

IN THE MONTPARNASSE CEMETERY

Those bells mean something, you said.

At first I barely hear them, think
they are the angelus from a nearby church

but the jangling clanging
insistence of the cemetery guards

ringing hand held brass bells
before closing the high iron gates

perambulating like monks
calling the friars to prayer

or sweeping the graveyard
of mortals before the sun sets.

Darkness falls—
the call awakens souls

like Beckett,
Baudelaire and Vallejo,

summoning them for their nightly
circumambulation.

Beckett casts a fishhook eye
on the rehearsal

asks the shadows
which of the shades is Godot?

Beaudelaire escapes his
family humming verses of Poe

seeks comfort
in the arms of Jeanne Duval.

Restive Vallejo longs only
for the snow capped Andes…

Whatever those peripatetic souls
rehearse or mumble

in prose or verse and even if
the tide of Paris traffic drowns

their crooning voices,
they will permit no living witness.

INVITATION

If I can believe in air, I can believe
in the angels of air.

Angels, come breathe with me.

Angel of abortion, angel of alchemy,
angels of barrenness & bliss,
exhale closer. Let me feel
your breath on my teeth—

I call to you, angels of embryos,
earthquakes, you of forgetfulness—

Angels of infection, cover my mouth
and nose with your mouth.

Failed inventions, tilt my head back.

Angels of prostitution and rain,
you of sheerness & sorrow,
you who take nothing,
breathe into me.

You who have cleansed your lips
with fire, I do not need to know
your faces, I do not need you
to have faces.

Angels of water insects, let me sleep
to the sound of your breathing.

You without lungs, make my chest rise—

without you my air tastes
like nothing. For you
I hold my breath.

KANSAS, 1973

My daughter nestled in a plastic seat
is nodding beside me as though in full
agreement with the logic of her dream.
I am glad for her sake the road is straight.
But the dark shimmer of a summer road
where hope and disappointment repeat
themselves all across Kansas like a dull
chorus makes the westward journey seem
itself a dream. She breathes in one great
gulp, taking deep the blazing air, and stops
my heart until she sighs the breath away.
The sun is stuck directly overhead.

I thought it all would never end. The drive,
the heat, my child beside me, the bright day
itself, that fathering time in my life.
We were going nowhere and never would,
as in a dream, or in the space between
time and memory. I saw nothing but sky
beyond the horizon of still treetops
and nothing changing down the road ahead.

LATE NAP

I take a long hot tub so that I can feel like a melon.
I dry myself off and tingle like a coral reef.
The lower sheet I pull up tight. I puff the pillows,

lie on my back, stretch out my arms and legs.
If I'm lucky, a breeze sweeps in sweet as silk.

The sleep is calm, like a coin at the bottom
of an old fortress wall that protrudes into the sea,
and the coin is almost green from the slow sloshing.

In the sleep, nobody comes after me, I don't
have to go anywhere, and I am immortal.

LETTER TO THE WINDING-SHEET

After the snowfall, snowfall
jewels my hair, my church shoes

muddy the bedspread. Crazy, you
called me, not much of a lady.

Flip up the light switch.
A child, I act a child.

At night I hold a postcard:
two plums adorn

a plum tree, what we could be.
The door tight in its door frame,

the window keeps
shutting on me.

In every dream I dream
I am asleep, your fingers

closed around my wrists.
Your breathing steals the room.

You won't explain my shrinking
vision, why I never knew enough

about the topiary—every limb
is a root, every tree a tree.

LOVE ARROW

Uncovering the street and you inside me, come to me
Quite how the other's leg
Thin golden skin closing firmly change that course
Fathoms beyond, if love brave
It's hard to change good people but no oh so allow
A pattern knocking—who are you? enraptured
You're a part of the world
Opens
A rusted silo deserves a tree growing love ants
Weep for me now

NIGHT LANDING

"I am giving up the landmarks by which I might be taking my bearings."
—Antoine de Saint-Expury, pilot

The hours that counted were measured by how much sand

was left in my pocket after charming you on the beach,
by the derivative of a voice over the single engine

as I remembered
back that far. You know,
time is not what I wanted—
fly past the horizon enough
and the moon on the starboard side
cuts visibility in half every time.
Besides, it's change in atmospheric pressure that's going to get us all in
 the end, anyway.

No, when hovering
over the Sargasso Sea
at night looking for landmarks,
it was etymology I wanted,

anthropological evidence it's not words that remain,
it's the space left when it quiets, the assumption of miracles.

And now it is morning
even though it is still dark,
it is morning—not last night, not last year,
it is morning.

On this earth it is always morning, somewhere.

NIGHT TRAIN

Daylight surrenders
to interior reflections
in a mottled collage
on the coach window.

My twin gazes back,
flickering as we race
through the fading
Van Gogh landscape.

Picking up speed,
we hurtle headlong
just above the track
verging on derailment.

We slam into darkness.
Plunged into silence,
I tunnel through granite,
pray for starlight.

OUR FLAG

should be green
to represent an ocean.
It should have two stars
in the first canton,
for us and navigation.
They should be of gold thread,
placed diagonally,
and not solid,
but comprised of lines.
Our flag should be silky jet.
It should have a wound,
a red river the sun must ford
when flown at half-mast.
It should have the first letter
of every alphabet ever.
When folded into a triangle
an embroidered eighth note
should rest on top
or an odd-pinnate,
with an argentine stem,
a fiery leaf, a small branch
signifying the impossible song.
Or maybe honey and blue
with a centered white pinion.
Our flag should be a veil
that makes the night weep
when it comes to dance,
a birthday present we open
upon death, the abyss we sleep
under. Our flag should hold
failure like light glinting
in a headdress of water.
It should hold the moon
as the severed head
of a white animal
and we should carry it
to hospitals and funerals,
to police stations and law offices.

It should live, divided,
deepening its yellows
and reds, flaunting itself
in a dead gray afternoon sky.
Our flag should be seen
at weddings well after
we've departed.
It should stir in the heat
above the tables and music.
It should watch our friends
join and separate
and laugh as they go out
under the clouded night
for cold air and cigarettes.
Our flag should sing
when we cannot,
praise when we cannot,
rejoice when we cannot.
Let it be a reminder.
Let it be the aperture,
the net, the rope of dark stars.
Let it be mathematics.
Let it be the eloquence
of the process shining
on the page, a beacon
on the edge of a continent.
Let its warnings be dismissed.
Let it be insignificant
and let its insignificance shine.

PAPER MILL

Below the basalt bluffs of Oregon City,
a steam punk circus of riveted acid skulls
spider-welded to the great skeleton of industry.
Rattling hoppers, cable-stayed stacks, iron steps up to a corrugated
    shack
where the pipe-fitters have coffee before tightening a clamp
on chip line number two.

God knows I use a lot of paper,
but there's something about a rusty red elbow
wrapped like a wound that makes me shiver back over the highway,
up to the faded blue Quonset of the American Legion's Post #5,
where Gus buys us beers.

World's first paper mill was in Bagdad, Gus tells me.
I'll be damned, another man says. If we could give up paper and oil we'd
    be all right.
We talk jobs and fishing, and how the old town is hanging on.
The young bartender with the prosthetic arm
says I should go upriver to Clackamas Park
and see those lampreys clinging to the rocks.

SOULS UNDER WATER

No longer tumbled by currents as when
long ago they were lodgers in frail bodies,
now they drift free of the flesh that was sucked
and nibbled from bones and the blood that swirled
away, its quick red streaking the deeps.

Souls mingle in the democracy of weed.
Passing through great barnacled bulkheads,
once-passengers, transparent without furs or jewels,
glide through the shiver that marks the presence
of stoker or convict, or the drunken oilman

who one night staggered to the edge of the spider-legged rig
and dreaming of his girlfriend—unusually tender
in his mind at that dizzy moment—plunged through cans
and plastic trash, into the arms of another.
Welcome, said the souls, though his ears heard nothing.

No longer sailors nor slaves, still they remember
the struck bell piercing sleep, the darkness
below decks where rats splashed in the bilges,
the wide-eyed newborn who flew over the deck rail
saved from the plantation by her mother's arm.

Oceans are thick with them: submariners floating
free of their vaults and pilots whose planes dropped
from the sky like giant guillemots but failed to surface
with a catch of fish. The careless were snatched
by sneaker waves, the joyful by cruising sharks

who dispatched them with a lunge and spat out
their splintered surfboards. Some are surprised
to find themselves here, having thought they'd ascend
to the heaven of upper airs or deep star space. But
these are the heavens, say the souls: the heavens below.

SUNDAY IS A SERIES OF HANDS

When leaves are tossed off
the roof in bags they hit
the ground like dead bodies
I put the thud in my chest
for later when I'll need it
The clouds have taken over
a monotonous haul
Your telescope is a metaphor
and anyway you can't use it here
Don't you feel it
Every broken thing just arrived
completely healed for the day
In this diorama you are
the tree and I am the same tree
We are making a stand
Miracles are rarely solvent
Every day a woman
inside the darkest shrine
rubs sacred dirt on her sorest parts
The sound she creates while praying
makes a mouse jealous
It starts to eat through the wall.

TANTALUS

The simplicity of the torture
was what always astonished him:
the receding lake of nakedness,
crispness of forbidden fruit.

Immortal, nourished on air
only his senses starved:
teeth in the apple,
hands in the clear water.

The final humiliation:
he envied Sisyphus
his boulder to lean on,
a sense of purpose.

THAT TIME AGAIN

east rain
new rain
bat out of hell rain
so dark I can't tell it's raining
step in it and don't get wet rain
what grows later
don't drink the rain
staining my glasses
eating away the tuna can I put out to measure it
b- d- t- rain
synthetic, fricative rain
rain hits the pavement so hard it rings
rain drops racing each other
sizzling rain
sweet & sour rain
rain across the street but not here
as if it's the first time rain has fallen
snake rain
steel drum rain
artisan rain
15.95 a pound rain
22 miles a gallon
rain like momma useta make
last rain
rain that can't decide which way to go
when two rain drops go through each other no one gets wet

THE BELLS OF ST. BAVO SING SCAT

Anticipating the lovers
who will soon be voices with bodies again,
the comforter on the bed fills with light
the color of sky when day puts up her feet and
slips on royal blue slippers.

Outside their window
the man on the roof dangles a dancing bear
or a baby grand or whatever
the lovers want to unhook and haul inside.

Finally, their bodies are fields
of yellow tulips fringed purple
slowly opening their fists,
the bells of St. Bavo singing scat,
fire-breathing dragons barreling out of children's books
to race through the streets of Haarlem.

Belts daddies used for beatings
stay in the loops of their pants.
Charred bodies resurrect themselves noticing
a faint smell of smoke in their sleek hair or
the tweed of their jackets, while lovers
who parted without declaring their love
feverishly lick stamps on envelopes
of yellowed love letters
or claw at blood-red wax seals.

THE END

it was the end of something,
and so we grew sad
according to how much we'd loved it.
now, nothing
but our great variety of sadnesses
and for some
a seed of instinct suggesting
something else
may eventually begin.

THE GIANTS

Out here, all darkness, stars overhead,
I can finally see the giants. After all the years
weighing dream's fragments, I can see
how each small thing, dead bees, a girl touching
her ear, rose petals in a pool of molasses, leads
to something larger than a life, the way the eye
follows a trail of stars then sees first one
and then another constellation against the dome
of night. My giants, I can almost love them now,
their hunger, like a piece of oak in the fire
eating every piece of wood around it,
they ate everything. They left the bones scattered
on the old brown sofa, the rabbit headless
in the yard. They lumbered, light full
on their shoulders, their hair backlit and flaming,
birds and small animals fleeing as whole families
left uneaten meals behind. I know
they can't eat me. I know them as I know
that to a child I might be as large as they were,
and when they fell, the distance of their falling
was so great the blood flowed, the earth
smoldered, and when they cried their crying
filled every room with their tears, and worst of all,
when they left they always came back,
the jostling, the trestles quaking
in those days of the giants sowing their bitter gifts,
their curses, their sour blessings, their hurled
and their spilled and their shattered. What was it
that ate them, the dream they couldn't see burning
inside them, the questions they never asked,
the tree whose shadow they did not lie down under?
I can see them, all that broke them, their shirts
creased with sweat and rank oil when they climbed
into the truck's cab at dusk clutching the brown bag
and the lottery ticket. Their feet rang out,
their doors slammed, they trudged, they cried,
they gave me these stars on a dark road, the rose book
on a winter afternoon, the hooked thorns

of the climbers, the ramblers blooming over walls
and outbuildings, blooming over their graves. They
gave me everything I wouldn't have known to love
without their whine, their roar, their terrible noise.

THE UNCLES

A haunted though thoroughly logical child,
I reasoned that yes, ghosts could terrify me,
but should one take a swipe with fist
or bloody chain, the ethereal blow
would just swish through my face. But the Devil,

Lucifer himself, roasted to a dark crimson
in the fires, his two horns like thorns
of a huge rose, he frightened me down
to my groin. I hated everyone completely.
Sins stained me, stuck to my fingers and palms

like pine pitch. There were not enough decades
of Joyful or Sorrowful Mysteries to see
me clear of damnation, an eternal
pressure cooker not for rattling jars
of sweet summer peaches but for my bones

and those of the equally luckless dead
locked forever in a roil of flame. To banish
the Devil, one must banish God, too,
a quid pro quo that began my long loneliness outside

the company of angels and saints. The day
I held open the secret backdoor of my soul
and said, you two must go, silent, they stood
up from their tea in the kitchen nook
and walked past me like two severe

yet frail uncles, each with a hitch
in the step, both disgusted and shamed,
back into the pagan forest, one a whiff
of mushroom, one a brush of morning breeze.

[THERE IS ANOTHER LIFE]

There is another life, only we are the same sweet sinners. I held her hand and listened when I wanted to. Outside, all the fumes of summer. She is for the ages, gathered from sugar and knives, beautiful cartoons of the flickering body. I never find out what my lies are for because I'm so tired in my favorite hours.

THERE WAS A WAR

and it wasn't ours because we didn't believe in it, and we didn't have guns, but they shot at us anyway because we existed somewhere in the middle of them killing each other. what could we do but lie still and wait? we lay a long time, the grass like trees shooting into the sky. bullets like bees shooting across it. too many hours of smoke in our eyes. we were thinking: if we had guns we'd use them to get the hell out of the middle of this war.

THRESHOLD:

where mothers prop themselves, welcoming, waving, mostly waiting. You are a frame your child passes through, the safest place to stand when the shaking starts. You brace yourself. He draws you like this, arms straight out, too stick-thin but the hands are perfect, splayed like suns, long fingers, the hands he draws for you are huge. Thresh, hold: separate the seeds, gather them back. In his pictures you all come close to holding hands, though the fingers of your family never touch; you're in the middle of all this reaching.

TINY ARCTIC ICE

Inhale, exhale
7 billion people breathing
Some of us in captivity
Our crops far-flung
Prison is a place where children sometimes visit
Jetted from Japan, edamame is eaten in England
Airplane air is hard to share
I breathe in what you breathe out, stranger
We send tea leaves to distant friends
Neighbors bike to build RVs at swing shift
Araucana chickens won't lay eggs in captivity
Airplanes of roses lift above Quito mountains
Cultivated from crocuses in La Mancha, saffron suffuses my rice
Status updates stack up in Prineville warehouses
Data, coal-powered and far-flung
When the fish diminish, folks find jobs in prisons
Sometimes children visit
Airplanes of microchips lift above Cascade mountains
Terminator seeds are hard to share
And the fish diminish
The roses, the tea, and the edamame, far-flung
The roses, the tea, the microchips, and you
You breathe in what I breathe out, friend

TO TAKE

I stole another woman's only scarf
and fed the calf and brushed its coat.
I tore the scarf to pieces and swore
I'd never leave the lake. The map of the lake
had a place marked by an arrow.
I buried the scarf there. I lived a little too close
to the shore and the pelicans gathered at
my back door. I emptied a bucket of fish
in the kitchen sink and opened the window wide.
Will you believe me when I say I didn't mean
to steal it? The scarf was hers, and no one there
to tell me not to take it. The pelicans
dived toward the window, but only one
made it in. The smallest one. Do you know
what happened then—how it filled its bill
with fish and flew back out the way
it came. The fish a gift for a bird that could
find enough to eat without me. The scarf
in pieces, buried near the lake with
other secrets kept nearby. I slept while the frogs
and flies sang back and forth their night time
songs. The lake was mine, the calf and pelican
safe in my keeping. I could knit another
scarf and leave it on her doorstep. I could
fill the sink with fish again. I was patient.
It was an accident, the way I took the scarf
when no one stood nearby.

VOICE OVER GUERILLAS

My body is a scar
The world starts us this way
always on the way out
of something
In my favorite movie
love is a snowball
and the screen is full
of wild dark hair
Stop and consider
the ethics of time
and give me an answer
The God particle
pastoralizes its reactor
until the trail is lost
in a riot of flowers
We all suspect everything
is an accident
on purpose
Existentially it's a toughie
But I finally did it
I met you
Isn't that enough

WAR AS THE CHERRY BLOSSOMS

We turn and turn and turn the soil of ourselves.

We prepare the same ancient armature.
The deception of language

is that we are beautiful, that we give and care

as the cherry blossoms
fall in the high heat of noon.

To think each moment
is new, that we are constantly beginning,
and what we do is what we have always done:

bury the dead in the vault of earth.

It's a disgrace.
We watch the season as it lets everything

rise and open.

Branches full of green. Our memory
that chain
we feel every time we walk.

WITHOUT

I drink from a glass without a rim
I stand on a ladder without rungs
I sleep in a bed with only my body,
my body from which the day's accumulations
drop away as I move in dreams
all night inside my solitude.

I ride the horse's back without a saddle
I pedal my bicycle with no hands.
No tongue, speechless, when I move into some thought
like an ice cave, slippery, forbidding.
I eat without chewing, food sliding
right past the guardian teeth. I make fires
without matches, swim without touching
a drop, see without light.
I find my way, make music
without notes, eyes closed, using both hands.

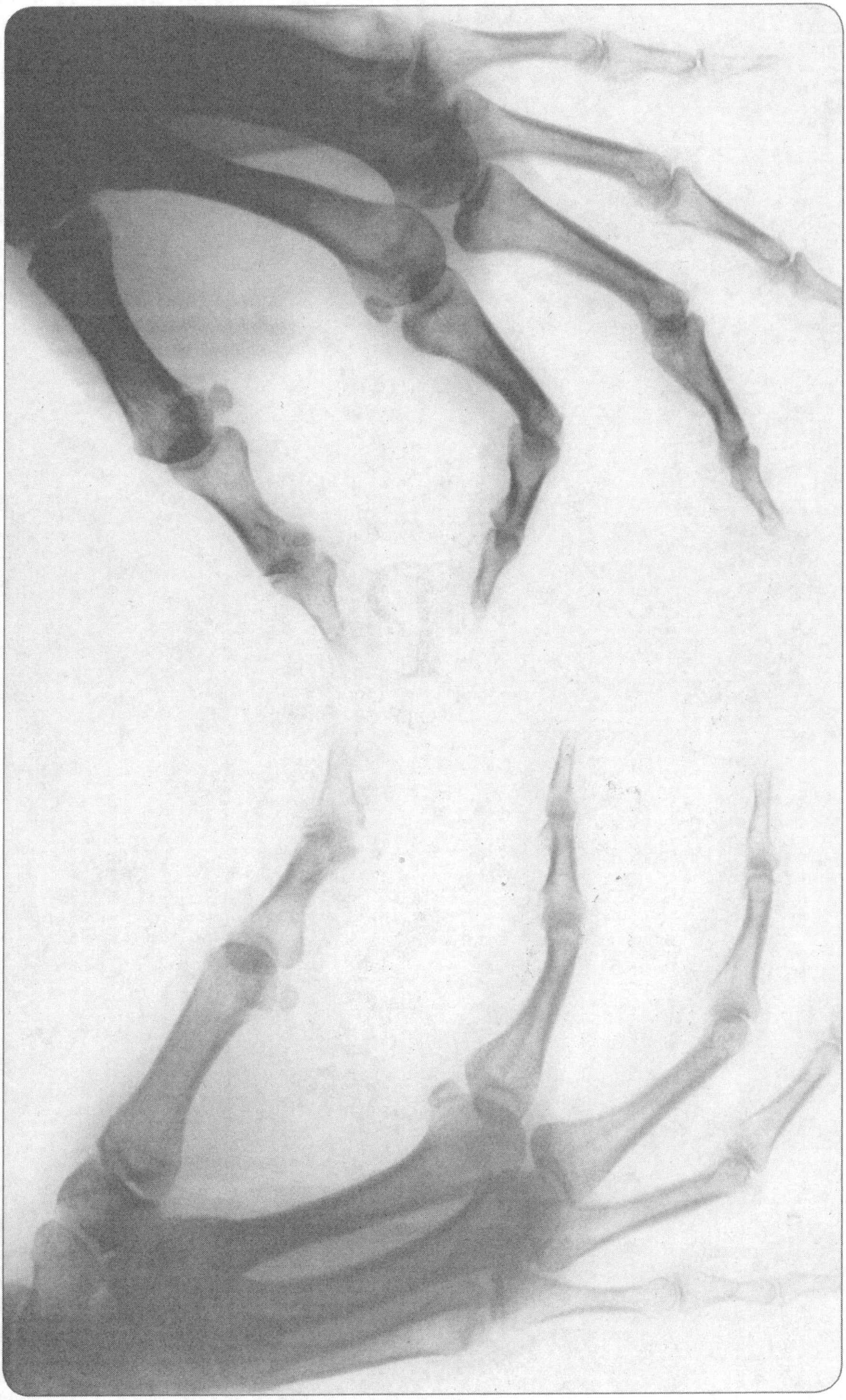

PACIFIC POETRY PROJECT

The Master's in Book Publishing at Portland State University, and Ooligan Press by extension, is a different sort of place. The students call the shots here, *learning* to publish books as they *actually* publish books. Part of our mission as a teaching institution is to teach not only our students, but our readers as well. What follows is a history of this project, *Alive at the Center*, from the graduate-student–project-manager perspective. These students follow the book along its path from acquisition to release and are intimately familiar with the book and all its personality traits. They have been kind enough to write their stories down so you, too, can be a part of the publishing process, from the student's perspective. I hope you enjoy its ups and downs, as I enjoy teaching through them, every day.

—Abbey Gaterud, Publisher

PACIFIC POETRY PROJECT – THE BEGINNING

The inspiration behind the Pacific Poetry Project (PPP) began in early 2010, when Ooligan Press editors expressed an interest in collaborating and publishing a new poetry collection. However, as so many regional poetry anthologies already exist, I asked the Acquisitions department (of which I was assistant manager) if I could run with a new idea, one that could stretch Ooligan's reach and potential influence beyond Oregon's borders, perhaps even America's borders.

Seattle, Washington, and Vancouver, British Columbia, are big-sister cities to Portland at heart—sharing so much culture and history, so many personalities and perspectives. I thought a literary collaboration between these Northwest artistic centers would build on this pre-existing bond.

First, the Acquisitions department hashed out a structure, creating regional editors and co-editors in order to expand the reach of the anthology. These regional editors would have their fingers on the pulse of their city, more so than Ooligan ever could. I then compiled lists of these poets and organization leaders and prepared templates for future communication with them. The list was long, as I knew some poets would be incommunicado or uninterested.

Next, I created a dozen-page marketing document, which I used to pitch the idea of PPP to the Ooligan Editorial Board. It included possible grant opportunities, social engagement ideas, and collaborations with arts organizations and government agencies. The plan brought the project's goal into focus: PPP should only contain poets who are actively involved in their local communities. This meant that the book (and therefore

Ooligan Press) would have dozens—perhaps a hundred—poets actively engaged with the book (and us) throughout the northwestern United States and British Columbia. The Editorial Board was excited by these ideas, and PPP was unanimously accepted.

Most exciting was when our publishers, Dennis and Abbey, suggested that PPP become a template for future books, serving as the first of many similar Ooligan anthologies. PPP would therefore establish Ooligan's own poetry 'brand' and series. With respect to marketing the book, it made sense to approach the endeavor as a social and cultural 'living' artifact, helping to keep it from becoming seen as "just another book on the shelf." With the help of Tony Anderson, I created a contact list of government agencies and literary organizations in the three cities, and contacted them to provide information about the publication and how it would benefit their cities. Our first time running this process, we focused on speaking of the book as a bridge between three communities.

Once accepted by Ooligan, volunteers from the Acquisitions department assisted me in contacting potential regional editors and booking all three cities. It was a difficult process but soon we confirmed the three teams of three editors for each city. We provided them with very specific guidelines and deadlines: they were given PPP's mission, scope, and marketing plan, as well as guidelines for the selection of poets within their cities. They understood what we wanted and how far we were willing to stretch our resources to help them. We knew that only collaboration could ensure the book and overall project would be a success.

After everyone was on board—all literary and government agencies were aware of the book, our social media campaign was solidified, the templates and plans were in place to ensure the participation of future editors, and all Ooligan departments were prepared—I stepped down from involvement in PPP and graduated from Portland State University.

PPP is my greatest achievement with Ooligan Press, and it was bittersweet to release my child into the world, to let it grow its own wings. I am also honored to have my own poetry within its pages, as one of the regional editors requested my work for inclusion.

—John Sibley Williams

FROM MANUSCRIPT TO TITLE TO COVER

Most Ooligan students manage a department or project at some point during their time in Ooligan. I signed up to be co-project manager for the Pacific Poetry Project. The previous term, I had worked with the Editing department on an initial read-through of the poems, to revise them and make queries to the authors. I was familiar with and enjoyed the content. We didn't have a title, which was necessary before the Design department could get started on a cover. As a title, Pacific Poetry Project wouldn't work. PPP was devised to be an Ooligan brand, anticipating future titles and external promotions.

In a brainstorming meeting, Abbey Gaterud (the publisher of Ooligan Press), suggested that we comb the poems for phrases that might make a fitting title. With highlighter in hand, that's exactly what I did. I went through all three regions (Portland, Seattle, and Vancouver): about 160 poems total. I made a list of forty phrases extracted from lines of the poems. Even taken completely out of context, some of these title contenders stood up surprisingly well. I knew I had too many possible titles to ever bring to a meeting, so I narrowed my forty down to twenty and threw them in a mass Ooligan survey. This way, my fellow students could help me determine a title.

The goal of developing the survey was to get students to read the poems and reflect on consistent themes and marketing ideas for the anthology. The question, "What should we avoid when designing the cover?" struck a chord. The consensus was that the press did not want any Pacific Northwest clichés (rain, rural settings, too much nature, abundance of the color green, etc.).

The poems ranged in setting. Many were urban, plenty were natural, but the majority shared a sense of melancholy and disillusionment. The most prevalent themes were light and darkness—both figuratively and literally. My co-manager (and now dear friend, thanks to the PPP project), Rachel Pass, helped me consolidate the responses. We then did some research, gabbed and honed our own ideas, and constructed a design brief. We sent it to the Design department so they could start thinking about covers. Still, they wouldn't have all the components necessary to build a solid cover until we had a solid title.

All Ooligan votes take place at Executive meetings, where everyone in the press has a chance to be heard. I'd prepared some notes for orchestrating a discussion regarding PPP's title. Based on feedback within the surveys and my own instincts, I'd narrowed the list down to ten possibilities. I put nine up on the dry erase board at the meeting, including one or two originals not taken from within lines of the poems, but suggested by students. I didn't realize how invested I was in the prosperity of this project until I heard myself talking about it.

I led the group down the list and we crossed out titles one by one. We examined the pros and cons of each contender: how it would or would not uphold the integrity of each poem and the collection as a whole; how it would appeal to or turn off readers; how it would represent the press and the three regions from which the poems hail; what would pop up online if someone did a search using the title's key words (a student sat with a laptop typing each possible title into Google, to ensure that nothing too raunchy would surface if we titled our anthology *Know the Trapdoors* or *Nothing Holds Like I Do*—real examples). The discussion was fun, and it got pretty intense, as Ooligan consists of passionate people with various tastes, experiences, and perspectives to offer.

Overall, students made it clear they did not want a title with an "I" in it, or anything too cryptic or interpretive, or anything quaint and romantic that could ever be the title to a country western song. An hour later, our list had shrunk to two, but everyone seemed to be a bit over those two prospects. Compromising is one thing, but settling is another. I knew I couldn't make all Ooliganites happy with one title, but I couldn't accept that everyone would leave the meeting uninspired. That's when I pulled out the kicker. Saying casually, "Oh look, I forgot this one—the tenth contender…" I wrote, *Alive at the Center* on the board. The room may as well have shaken with the shift in enthusiasm. We were rejuvenated and within seconds, the time it took me to count the "yays" and "nays," it was all over. All but two hands out of a fifty were up in the final vote for this title contender.

The front cover for our anthology was inspired by this title and designed by one of Ooligan's talented students, J. Adam Collins. By restricting the color, there is a subliminal feeling of harmony between the image and the semantics of the title. The eye-catching, haunting image of the skeletal fingers and the vibrant bird in flight creates a provocative intrigue. Heavy with symbolism, the fingers signify the life as well as the dormant death within us.

The x-ray reference evokes the role of the machine, which speaks to our modern world. We don't actually see the machine, just the result—that is, our bones. In this way the hands are pure, organic, and relatable. In context with the hands, the image of the bird is nature reinvented, and the movement captured is a visceral one. The image also thrives within the tension between the forms. Is this bird about to be crushed or cradled? Perhaps the most accurate answer is, "both," as people will see what they want to see, and either perception sparks an emotional reaction.

With all due respect, I find the majority of poetry anthologies have forgettable covers, though the content may be anything but. Ooligan needed this unforgettable cover to represent the words within. The only risk would have been *not taking a risk* on this maverick design. I believe it will command attention on any bookshelf.

—*Amber May*

FROM PERMISSIONS TO GALLEYS AND BEYOND

Like Amber, I came to work on the Pacific Poetry Project in January of 2012, just before the title was chosen and the cover was designed. I was scared stiff when I volunteered for the job. I had no idea how I would juggle a management role at the press while working and taking classes. However, within a week of starting the job, I learned two invaluable things:

1. All Ooligonians are in the same busy position, so I had no right to whine.
2. The best way to get your feet wet at the press is to dive in headfirst and start swimming.

At Ooligan, this means braving a steady current of meetings, e-mails, and friendly debates; all the while gauging the pull of Ooligan's separate book projects—each project acts as a separate moon and creates complicated tides. At first this was overwhelming. But once I became familiar with the work, I saw that I wouldn't sink if I reached out for help when the current got too strong. Everyone at Ooligan is ready and willing to help.

As soon as I was comfortable in my position, I realized what an incredible opportunity I had been handed. The Pacific Poetry Project is a huge risk with a huge heart. In its mission to seek out and connect the myriad poets of the Northwest's three largest cities in a borderless artistic community, it has tested the considerable abilities of all the departments in our press community.

Many challenging tasks made the Pacific Poetry Project a success. We have had to keep an extensive database for permissions, documenting whether or not we could legally print the more than 200 poems submitted by over 160 poets. We designed and created four separate covers—one for the anthology, and three equally stunning covers for the individual city editions. Marketing and promoting these beautiful books involved everything from a grass-roots reading series to an extensive online presence; a conference with national sales representatives assured that we will have booksellers throughout and beyond the Northwest on board when the book goes live.

There have been struggles along the way. Some production deadlines flew by unmet, some technology demons crept up and ate the occasional document, and some debates grew too heated. But that is the way of any press. I'm proud to say that throughout the past two and a half years since the book's conception, no problem has arisen that the press hasn't been able to band together to solve.

It is now July of 2012. Jonathan Stark and I are the project's current co-managers. We are in the privileged position of looking back and admiring the incredible amount of work that has been done to bring *Alive at the Center*, the first installment of the Pacific Poetry Project series, to fruition.

There is, however, no treading water at Ooligan as there is always more work to be done. Next month we will send out copies for review and our Editing department will apply for *Alive at the Center*'s official library listing from the Library of Congress. In light of all of this we want to thank everyone within and outside of the press who has had a hand in this project to date, as well as those who will step in to plan and execute the separate city launches. Thank you, for making sure this book finds its well-deserved community of readers, who will love it as much as we do.

—Rachel Pass

THE PROJECT NEVER ENDS

My first involvement in the Pacific Poetry Project was to suggest a title to Amber May: *Stealing Home Again.* Thankfully, despite the complicated metaphor which informed my suggestion, it wasn't chosen. Heck, I voted for *Alive at the Center.* That could have marked the extent of my involvement with the project, but a term later Amber retired from being its project manager and a need for someone to take her spot was created. I tentatively signed up.

I say tentative not because I was wary of the project. Actually, the chance to work on a poetry anthology seemed a very unique one, and exciting. Certainly it was outside of the norm for your usual graduate school work. I was more concerned with my lack of experience in the press. This was only my second term. The Pacific Poetry Project already had a rich and tumultuous history behind it, spanning back to 2010. I was introduced to this history by Rachel Pass in a flurry of explanations, Google documents, and meetings with people who seemed to genuinely believe I knew the answers to their questions. Continuing Rachel's metaphor, I questioned my ability to be able to navigate these choppy waters. When it comes to water, I am, at best, a decent doggy-paddler.

So I doggy-paddled. And I tried to keep the shoreline in sight.

I won't lie—working on *Alive at the Center* was overwhelming at times. It was also exhilarating. Being counted on to bring something to success can show you a determination you didn't know you had. In the course of my work I learned some valuable lessons about project management. Always smile. Approach every person you work with as if they were a close friend and soon they will be. Tackle every problem with a full heart and an open mind. Remember that you are not the first person to paddle these waters, nor will you be the last. After all...

...the project never ends.

When we sweat and bleed over something, a piece of ourselves is imprinted on it. In this way, it is hard for me to move on from *Alive at the Center,* because there's a bit of me in its pages. But it is now time to pass the project on once again—this time to you, the reader.

One of the wonderful things about poetry is that it is not a static art form. It does not tell one story set in stone, but rather tells as many stories as exist in our hearts. Poetry is an active language, which asks us to interact with its every word and carefully arranged syllables. The readers will be the new project managers of *Alive at the Center*, reinterpreting it every time they browse its pages, adding their own thoughts and imprinting their own meaning on each poem. In doing this, readers will become a part of the project's history, expanding it far beyond the horizon that everyone who worked on it swam towards. Take this project, own it, and approach it with heart and smiles.

And happy paddling.

—Jonathan Stark

If you enjoyed reading about this book's story, check out the Start to Finish project on the Ooligan Press website: www.ooliganpress.pdx.edu

VANCOUVER

Aislinn Hunter is the author of two books of poetry (*Into the Early Hours* and *The Possible Past*), two works of fiction (*What's Left Us* and *Stay*), and a book of lyric essays on "thing theory" (*A Peepshow with Views of the Interior: Paratexts*). She is currently finishing her PhD on Victorian writers and resonant objects at the University of Edinburgh. Her primary subject is the past and the importance of history—even in its fractured, fragmented and unreliable forms.

Twenty-six-year-old **Alex Winstanley** lives in Vancouver, British Columbia, where he is pursuing a career as a professional writer and ESL teacher. He recently graduated with a BA in religion and literature at the University of British Columbia. The son of a Mexican mother and English father, Alexander's poetry reflects the dual nature of his origins, which allows him the freedom to explore different philosophies. His new book of poetry, *The Bones in Our Wings*, immerses the imagination in ideas of reincarnation.

Andrea Bennett writes poetry, fiction, and non-fiction. Her work has appeared in several Canadian literary journals and cultural magazines. She was recently nominated for a National Magazine Award and the Journey Prize, and has previously been shortlisted for the 2010 and 2011 Matrix Litpop Awards, as well as the 2011 *EVENT Magazine* Nonfiction Contest. She is an associate editor at *Adbusters Magazine*, the News Columns Editor at *This Magazine*, and she moonlights at *PRISM international*.

Anna Swanson is a poet and children's librarian living in Vancouver, British Columbia. Her debut book of poetry, *The Nights Also*, questions how identity is formed and challenged in relation to chronic illness, sexuality, and solitude. It won a Lambda Literary Award and the Gerald Lampert Memorial Award.

Bonnie Nish is the founder of Twisted Poets Open Mic, and co-founder of both Pandora's Collective and The Kitsilano Writing Group (writing collectives in Vancouver, British Columbia). A captivating storyteller, Bonnie allows us to see the world in a slightly unique way, presenting a refreshing view of life through her poetry. Published widely throughout North America, you may view some of her work in the anthologies *Undercurrents* and *Quills*, and online at hack writers and Greenboathouse Press.

Bren Simmers lives in Vancouver, British Columbia, where she works as a park interpreter. She was a recipient of the *Arc Poetry Magazine* Poem of the Year Award, and a finalist for the RBC Bronwen Wallace Award for Emerging Writers and *The Malahat Review* Long Poem Prize. Her first book of poems, *Night Gears*, was published by Wolsak and Wynn in 2010. She is currently working on a cycle of poems about seasonal and cultural changes in her East Van neighborhood.

Carl Leggo is a poet and professor in the Department of Language and Literacy Education at the University of British Columbia. His books include: *Growing Up Perpendicular on the Side of a Hill; View from My Mother's House; Come-By-Chance;* and *Teaching to Wonder: Responding to Poetry in the Secondary Classroom*. Integral to his creative and academic life, Carl is a happy grandfather to three darling granddaughters with the magical names Madeleine, Mirabelle, and Gwenoviere.

Catherine Owen is a poet, writer, and musician based out of Vancouver, British Columbia. She's been writing poetry since she was three, performing from the age of eighteen, and publishing since the age of twenty-one. The author of nine collections of poetry and one of prose, she's been nominated for awards such as the Air Canada/CBC Poetry Prize, ReLit Award, and the BC Book Prize. Her book, *Frenzy*, won the 2009 Alberta Book Award.

Chris Gilpin is a spoken word performer, videographer, and arts educator living in Vancouver, British Columbia. He is the 2012 Nerd Slam champion and the 2012 Erotica Slam champion. He is also a two-time member of the Vancouver Poetry Slam Team (2008 and 2009), and the winner of Vancouver's 2008 Haiku Death Match, Vancouver's 2009 CBC Poetry Face-off, and the 2011 Vancouver Individual Poetry Slam. His literary work has been published in *Geist*, and *PRISM international*, among others.

Christi Kramer, a PhD candidate at the University of British Columbia, specializing in poetic imagination and peace building, holds an MFA from George Mason University and a BA from Linfield College in Oregon. Deeply in love with the landscapes of the Pacific Northwest, Christi lives both in Vancouver, British Columbia, and in northern Idaho where she was born.

Originally from London, England, **Christopher Levenson** lived and taught English and Creative Writing at Carleton University, Ottawa from 1968 until his retirement in 1999. Christopher has published ten books of poetry and edited three poetry anthologies. He is also the co-founder and first editor of *Arc Poetry Magazine*, as well as series editor of the Harbinger Poetry Series of Carleton University Press. His latest book, *Night Vision*, will appear with Quattro Press, Toronto, in fall of 2013.

Daniela Elza has lived on three continents and crossed numerous geographic, cultural, and semantic borders; her interests lie in the gaps, rubs, and bridges between poetry, language, and philosophy. Poetry for her is a way of life, a way of loosening our grip on the world to allow for a more intimate connection with it. Daniela has more than 200 poems published in over fifty publications, with her second book (through Leaf Press) slated for a fall 2013 release. In 2011, she completed her PhD in Philosophy of Education and launched her first eBook, *the book of It*.

David Zieroth's most recent book of poetry, *The Fly in Autumn* (Harbour), won the Governor General's Literary Award in 2009 and was nominated for the Dorothy Livesay Poetry Prize and the Acorn-Plantos Award for People's Poetry in 2010. He won the Dorothy Livesay Poetry Prize for *How I Joined Humanity at Last* (Harbour, 1998). He founded The Alfred Gustav Press, a micro press for publishing poetry, in 2008. He lives in North Vancouver, British Columbia.

Dennis E. Bolen—a novelist, editor, teacher and journalist—was first published in 1975 in Canadian Fiction Magazine. He holds a BA in Creative Writing from the University of Victoria (1977) and an MFA in Writing from the University of British Columbia (1989), and taught introductory Creative Writing at UBC from 1995–1997. His seventh book of fiction, *Anticipated Results*, was published by Arsenal/Pulp Press in April 2011.

Diane Tucker was born and raised in Vancouver, British Columbia, where she earned a BFA from the University of British Columbia in 1987. *God on His Haunches*, her first book of poetry, was published by Nightwood Editions in 1996. It was shortlisted for the 1997 Gerald Lampert Memorial Award. Her second book of poems, *The Bright Scarves of Hours*, was published in September of 2007 by Palimpsest Press. Her poems have been published internationally in more than sixty journals.

Elee Kraljii Gardiner directs Thursdays Writing Collective, a nonprofit program in downtown eastside Vancouver, British Columbia. She is the editor of five chapbooks and the co-editor (alongside John Asfour) of *V6A: Writing from Vancouver's Downtown Eastside*, an anthology from Arsenal Pulp Press (2012). Elee holds an MA in Hispanic Studies from the University of British Columbia and is affiliated with Simon Fraser University, sitting on the Advisory Council of The Writer's Studio.

Evelyn Lau is an internationally known Vancouver, British Columbia, writer who has published ten books, including five volumes of poetry. *You Are Not Who You Claim* won the Milton Acorn Award; *Oedipal Dreams* was nominated for a Governor-General's Award. Her poems have been included in the *Best American Poetry* and *Best Canadian Poetry* anthologies, as well as receiving a National Magazine Award. Her most recent collection, *Living Under Plastic* (Oolichan, 2010), won the Pat Lowther Memorial Award. She is currently Poet Laureate for the city of Vancouver, where she freelances as a manuscript consultant in Simon Fraser University's Writing and Publishing Program.

Fran Bourassa is a poet, workshop facilitator, and contributing writer to numerous anthologies. She was awarded a scholarship to The Banff Centre's Wired Writing Studio and has twice been a delegate for the British Columbia Festival of the Arts. She also took first place in the 2011 Vancouver International Writers Festival poetry contest.

Garry Thomas Morse is the author of *Transversals for Orpheus, Streams, Death in Vancouver, After Jack* (an homage to Jack Spicer), and *Discovery Passages,* the first collection of poetry about the Kwakwaka'wakw (Kwakiutl) First Nations people. His second book of fiction is *Minor Episodes / Major Ruckus* from Talonbooks.

George McWhirter became Vancouver, British Columbia's, inaugural Poet Laureate in 2007. He has published ten books of poetry, his most recent being *The Anachronicles* (Ronsdale Press, 2008). He is a Commonwealth Poetry Prize winner and was awarded the F.R. Scott Translation Award for the *José Emilio Pacheco: Selected Poems.*

Heather Haley, "The Siren of Howe Sound," is a trailblazing poet, author, musician, and media artist who pushes boundaries by creatively integrating disciplines, genres, and media. She has been published in numerous journals, anthologies, and collections—including *Sideways* (Anvil Press) and *Three Blocks West of Wonderland* (Ekstasis Editions).

Heidi Greco is an editor and writer whose poems have appeared in a range of magazines and anthologies. She also writes book reviews for newspapers and magazines. Heidi lives in South Surrey, British Columbia, in a house surrounded by trees. Heidi was a participant in the first Cascadia Poetry Festival, a trans-border celebration of the spoken word. Heidi keeps a sporadic blog entitled *out on the big limb.*

Ibrahim Honjo is a poet/writer, sculptor, painter, photographer, and property manager. His work can be found within numerous magazines, newspapers, and on the radio. Honjo has authored twelve books, contributed to four anthologies, and received several poetry prizes. His poetry has been translated in Korean, Slovenian, and German.

Jason Sunder lives in Vancouver, British Columbia. His poetry has appeared in *OCW Magazine, Ampersand*, and *The Maynard*. A chapbook is forthcoming.

Born and raised in Portland, Oregon, **Jen Currin** currently lives in Vancouver, British Columbia, where she teaches creative writing at Kwantlen University and for Simon Fraser University's Writer's Studio. Jen has published three books of poems: *The Sleep of Four Cities* (2005), *Hagiography* (2008), and *The Inquisition Yours* (2010), which was a finalist for the ReLit Poetry Award, a Lambda Literary Award, and the Dorothy Livesay Poetry Prize. It won The Audre Lorde Award for Lesbian Poetry.

Joanne Arnott is a Métis/mixed-blood writer & arts activist. She grew up in East Vancouver, British Columbia, and returned to stay in 1982. She volunteers for national and local literary organizations, currently The Writers Trust of Canada and Aboriginal Writers Collective West Coast, and participates in international literary projects. Her published work includes *Breasting the Waves: On Writing & Healing* (1995), *Mother Time: Poems New & Selected* (2007), and the poetry chapbook *the family of crow* (2012).

Kagan Goh was born in Singapore in 1969. After years of traveling, he migrated to Canada in 1986 and now resides in Vancouver, British Columbia. He is an award-winning documentary filmmaker, a spoken-word poet, novelist, journalist and mental health activist. His work has been published in anthologies such as *Strike the Wok: an Anthology of Contemporary Chinese Canadian Fiction* (TSAR Publications) and *Henry Chow and Other Stories from the Asian Canadian Writer's Workshop* (Tradewinds Books). *Who Let In the Sky?* is his first book. It is a memoir about his father's struggle with Parkinson's disease and eventual death.

Kate Braid has written poetry and non-fiction about subjects from Glenn Gould and Emily Carr to mine workers and fishers. She has published five books of prize-winning poetry, most recently, *Turning Left to the Ladies* and *A Well-Mannered Storm: The Glenn Gould Poems.*

Kevin Spenst's poetry has either appeared in or is forthcoming from *Rhubarb Magazine, Capilano Review, The Maynard, Ditch Poetry, four and twenty, and* OCW *Magazine*. In 2011 his manuscript *The Gang's All Down by the Abecedarium* was shortlisted for the Robert Kroetsch Award for Innovative Poetry. Most recently, he won Vancouver's second annual Literary Death Match.

Kim Fu's poetry has appeared in *Grain, Room, The New Quarterly, Numero Cinq*, and on CBC Radio. Her debut novel, *For Today I Am a Boy*, will be published in 2013 with Houghton Mifflin Harcourt, HarperCollins Canada, and Random House Australia. Her literary nonfiction has been nominated for a National Magazine Award and won second prize in the 2010 Prairie Fire contest. She holds an MFA from the University of British Columbia.

Lilija Valis, born in Lithuania, has lived on three continents during times of war and peace, riots and festivals. While pursuing education and working in cities across America—from Boston and New York to San Francisco—she participated in programs that help to liberate people from poverty and personal misery. Her poetry has been included in two anthologies and her book *Freedom On the Fault Line* was published in 2012.

Lucia Misch grew up at an astronomical observatory in California, and has been writing and performing spoken word in—and around—the state since she was fifteen. She was the 2007 and 2008 South Bay Youth Slam Champion, and has had the honor of being part of three San Jose youth teams. She moved to Vancouver, British Columbia, and has maintained a strong presence there ever since. She was a member of the 2010 Slam Team and placed second at the Canadian Individual Poetry Slam Championship in April 2012.

Marni Norwich is a Vancouver, British Columbia, writer, editor, writing workshop facilitator, and author of the poetry collection *Wildflowers At My Doorstep* (Karma Press, 2008). She's been reading and performing on Vancouver stages for eight years, sometimes with the accompaniment of dancers, choreographers and musicians.

Natasha Boskic lives in Vancouver, British Columbia, and writes both poetry and short stories. She likes experimenting with new technologies as she is fascinated by the opportunities they represent. As a result her poetry is often an exciting encounter of audio, video, and text. She writes in English and Serbian.

Poet, editor, and artist **Nikki Reimer** is the author of *[sic]* (Frontenac House, 2010), and the chapbooks *haute action material* (Heavy Industries, 2010) and *fist things first* (Wrinkle Press Chapbook, 2009). Another chapbook, *that stays news*, is forthcoming from Nomados Press. Reimer lives, works, and writes in Vancouver, British Columbia.

Onjana Yawnghwe has been featured in a number of Canadian literary journals and anthologies. Her most recent work includes the JackPine chapbook *The Imaginary Lives of Buster Keaton*, and the anthology *4 Poets* (MotherTongue Publishing). She lives in Burnaby with a tortoiseshell and a librarian.

Rachel Rose has won awards for her poetry, her fiction, and her nonfiction. She has published poems, short stories, and essays in Canada, the United States, New Zealand, and Japan, in publications such as *Poetry*, *The Malahat Review*, and *The Best American Poetry.* She is the author of two books, teaches at Simon Fraser University, and is the founder of the "Cross-Border Pollination" reading series, bringing Canadian and American writers together to read in Vancouver.

Raoul Fernandes lives and writes in Vancouver, British Columbia. He completed The Writer's Studio in 2009 and was a finalist for this year's RBC Bronwen Wallace Award for Emerging Writers. He is currently working on his first poetry manuscript. You can read his blog at raoulfernandes.com

Renée Sarojini Saklikar writes *The Canada Project*, about life from India to Canada's west coast, and places in between. Work from The Canada Project appears in various literary journals and anthologies. Long poems and fiction from The Canada Project have been short-listed for national awards.

Rita Wong is the author of three books of poetry. She received the Asian Canadian Writers Workshop Emerging Writer Award in 1997, and the Dorothy Livesay Poetry Prize in 2008. Building from her doctoral dissertation, which examined labor in Asian North American literature, her work investigates the relationships between contemporary poetics, social justice, ecology, and decolonization.

Rob Taylor's first book of poetry, *The Other Side of Ourselves*, was published in April 2011 by Cormorant Books. Prior to publication, the manuscript for the book won the 2010 Alfred G. Bailey Poetry Prize. Rob has also published three chapbooks and his poems have appeared in over forty journals, magazines, and anthologies. In 2004, he co-founded Simon Fraser University's student poetry zine *High Altitude Poetry*, and in 2007 he co-founded *One Ghana, One Voice*, Ghana's first online poetry magazine.

Robin Susanto is a mathematician by training. He resorts to poetry when things don't add up. Born in Indonesia, he now writes and mathematizes in Vancouver. His poetry can be found in journals including *Quills Canadian Poetry Magazine, BluePrintReview,* and *qarrtsiluni,* as well as XXX, an anthology of love poems published by Leaf Press. His translation of a 1928 Indonesian novel was published by the Lontar Foundation under the title *Never the Twain.*

Russell Thornton's books include *House Built of Rain* (Harbour, 2003)—which was nominated for the ReLit Poetry Award and the Dorothy Livesay Poetry Prize. Thornton obtained an MA from Simon Fraser University, and for a number of years divided his life between Vancouver, British Columbia and Aberystwyth, Wales, and then Salonica, Greece. He now lives where he was born and grew up, in North Vancouver, at the foot of the mountains on the north shore of Burrard Inlet.

Sandy Shreve has published four poetry collections, her most recent being *Suddenly, So Much* (Exile Editions, 2005). She also founded British Columbia's Poetry in Transit program. Her work is widely anthologized and has won or been shortlisted for a variety of poetry awards.

Shannon Rayne is a Vancouver, British Columbia, poet. Her poems appear in the *Feathertale Review, Filling Station, Poetry is Dead* and in a recent anthology by Ferno House Press featuring erotic poetry about dinosaurs. Her poems have been recently interpreted by composers and mixed media artists. She is currently working on two manuscripts, *Dirty* and *Coffee Stained Poems*.

Susan Cormier—a.k.a. Queen of Crows—is a multimedia writer working in print, performance, and audio-video recording. She has won or been shortlisted for such awards as CBC's National Literary Award, *Arc Magazine*'s Poem of the Year, and the Federation of BC Writers' Literary Writes. She lives in East Vancouver.

Susan McCaslin is a prizewinning Canadian poet and educator who received her PhD in English from the University of British Columbia, and taught English and Creative Writing at Douglas College in New Westminster, British Columbia from 1984–2007. Her work has appeared in literary journals across Canada and the United States. She has published eleven volumes of poetry, eight poetry chapbooks, many academic articles, essays, and a children's book.

Susan Musgrave's most recent collection of poetry is *Origami Dove* (M&S, 2011). She lives on Haida Gwaii and teaches poetry in the University of British Columbia's Optional Residency in Creative Writing program.

Taryn Hubbard is a writer from Vancouver, British Columbia, interested in "exploring technology, social and lived spaces through poetry and photography." She has been published in CV2, *subTerrain,* OCW *Magazine,* and *Trickhouse.* She studied English and Creative Writing at Simon Fraser University, and journalism at Langara College. A collective member of The Storytelling Show on Vancouver Co-op Radio (102.7 FM), Taryn teaches creative writing workshops within the community.

Timothy Shay writes and lives in Vancouver, British Columbia. His work has appeared in many Canadian literary magazines, on CBC Radio, and in *Rolling Stone.* He has one collection of poetry, *This Cabin As The SS Titanic,* and several chapbooks. Timothy Shay hosts two events for writers in Vancouver: Hogan's Alley Open Poetry Readings, which are held once a month at Hogan's Alley Cafe, and the Twisted Poets Literary Salon, a Pandora's Collective event held at the Prophouse Cafe twice each month.

Poet, critic and literary journalist **Trevor Carolan** has travelled internationally for more than thirty years, writing on art, literature, music, politics, and Asian cultures. His publications include many books and his work has appeared in five languages. He teaches English and Creative Writing at University of the Fraser Valley, British Columbia.

SEATTLE

Belle Randall grew up in the Bay Area and attended the University of California, Berkeley, where her freshman English teacher was Thom Gunn, who became a lifelong friend until his death in 2004. For twenty years (1982–2002) Belle herself taught literature at Cornish College of the Arts in Seattle. Now retired from teaching, Belle continues to write and be active in the Seattle poetry scene. Her poems and essays have appeared in numerous publications, including *Poetry* and *The Threepenny Review*.

Brian Culhane, a writer and teacher, was the recipient of the Poetry Foundation's Emily Dickinson First Book Award—a prize given to a first collection written by a poet over the age of fifty—for his 2008 book *The King's Question*. Brian's poems have appeared in a number of journals, including *The New Republic* and *The Paris Review.* He holds a PhD in Epic Literature and the History of Criticism from the University of Washington.

Carol Light's poems have appeared in *Prairie Schooner* and *Mare Nostrum*. She earned her MFA from the University of Washington and teaches middle school on the Olympic Peninsula. She lives in Port Townsend, Washington, with her family.

Christianne Balk's books include *Bindweed* (Macmillan, recipient of the Walt Whitman Award), and *Desiring Flight* (Purdue University Press). She loves broken music, the haunting Anglo-British Columbia Saxon rhythms of everyday street talk, and riding her mother-in-law's thirty-year-old bike in triathlons. After majoring in biology at Grinnell College, she studied English at the University of Iowa. Her work has appeared in *The Alaska Quarterly Review* and *The Atlantic Monthly,* among others. She lives in Seattle with her husband and daughter.

Christine Deavel was born in North Manchester, Indiana, and graduated from Indiana University and the University of Iowa. She is co-owner of Open Books: A Poem Emporium and lives in Seattle.

Cody Walker's first poetry collection, *Shuffle and Breakdown*, was published by The Waywiser Press in 2008. His awards include the James Boatwright III Prize for Poetry from Shenandoah and residency fellowships from the University of Arizona Poetry Center, the Amy Clampitt Fund, and the Sewanee Writers' Conference. A longtime writer-in-residence in Seattle Arts & Lectures' Writers in the Schools program, he was elected Seattle Poet Populist in 2007.

David D. Horowitz founded and manages Rose Alley Press, which primarily publishes books featuring contemporary Northwest rhymed metrical poetry. Many of his poems have been published in literary journals such as *The Lyric*, *Candelabrum*, and *The New Formalist*. In 2005, David won the PoetsWest Achievement Award. David gives frequent readings in and around Seattle, where he lives.

Deborah Woodard's "Hamlet Mnemonic Series" won the Chelsea Award for Poetry for 2007. In collaboration with Giuseppe Leporace, she has translated the distinguished modernist Italian poet, Amelia Rosselli. Deborah teaches at Richard Hugo House, a community literary center in Seattle.

Derek Sheffield's collection, *A Revised Account of the West*, won the inaugural Hazel Lipa Environmental Chapbook Award in 2008, and was judged by Debra Marquart. His poems have also appeared in *Poetry*, *Orion*, and *The Southern Review*, among others. In 2012, he was awarded a fellowship from Artist Trust and his full-length collection was runner-up for the Emily Dickinson First Book Award.

Ed Skoog is the author of two books of poems published by Copper Canyon Press, *Mister Skylight* (2009) and *Rough Day* (2013). His poems have been published in *The Paris Review*, *The American Poetry Review*, and *Poetry*, among others. He grew up in Topeka, Kansas, got an MFA from the University of Montana, and lived in Seattle in the mid-nineties. He moved to New Orleans for a long stretch, but returned to Seattle in 2008.

Elizabeth Austen is the author of *Every Dress a Decision* (Blue Begonia Press, 2011), and two chapbooks, including *Where Currents Meet* (one of four winners of the 2010 Toadlily Press chapbook award and part of the quartet *Sightline*). Her poems have been featured on Garrison Keillor's *The Writer's Almanac* and *Verse Daily*, in journals including the *Los Angeles Review*, and in anthologies, including *Fire on Her Tongue* and *Poets Against the War*. Her work has twice been nominated for the Pushcart prize.

Emily Beyer lives and works in Seattle. Her poems have appeared in *The Seattle Review*, *Mare Nostrum*, and *Prairie Schooner*, among others. Along with writing poetry, she has taught poetry and writing classes to adults and children for more than nine years.

For **Emily Warn**, poetry links music and meaning every bit as powerfully and oddly as religious traditions do, inventing complicated, invisible relations. Warn's newest collection of poetry is *Shadow Architect* (Copper Canyon Press, 2008). Her previous books include *The Leaf Path* (Copper Canyon Press, 1982) and *The Novice Insomniac* (Copper Canyon Press, 1996). She currently lives in Seattle.

Frances McCue is a poet, essayist, reviewer, and arts instigator. From 1996–2006, she was the founding director of Richard Hugo House in Seattle. In 2011, McCue became the first writer to win the Washington State Book Award for Poetry (*The Bled*) and place as a finalist for a second book (*The Car That Brought You Here Still Runs*) during the same year. *The Bled* also won the Grub Street National Book Prize. Her first poetry collection, *The Stenographer's Breakfast*, won the Barnard New Women's Poetry Prize.

Heather McHugh—poet, translator, and educator—was born in San Diego, California, to Canadian parents who would eventually raise her in Gloucester Point, Virginia. She began writing poetry at age five and claims to have become an expert eavesdropper by the age of twelve. At the age of seventeen, she entered Harvard University. Her most notable work was *Hinge & Sign: Poems 1968–1993*, which won the Bingham Poetry Prize of the Boston Book Review and the Pollack-Harvard Review Prize.

A finalist for the 2003 Arts & Letters Prize, **Holly J. Hughes**' poems have appeared in such journals as *The Midwest Quarterly*, and *Americas Review*, as well as in the anthology, *American Zen: A Gathering of Poets*. Her essays have appeared in *Crosscurrents* and the anthology *Steady As She Goes: Women's Adventures at Sea*. She has taught writing at Edmonds Community College for more than fifteen years, serving as co-advisor to the college's award-winning literary/art journal, *Between the Lines*.

J.W. Marshall co-owns and operates Open Books, with his wife Christine Deavel. Open Books is a poetry-only bookstore in Seattle that the couple established in 1995. His first full-length collection of poetry, *Meaning a Cloud*, won the Field Poetry Prize and was published in 2008 by Oberlin College Press. He holds an MFA from the Iowa Writers Workshop (1984), as well as an MA in Rehabilitation Counseling from Seattle University (1986).

Jared Leising is the author of a chapbook of poems—*The Widows and Orphans of Winesburg, Ohio*—and, in 2010, Jared curated the Jack Straw Writers Program. He's served as president of the Washington Community

College Humanities Association and on the Board of Directors for 826 Seattle. Before moving to Seattle, Jared received his MFA in Creative Writing from the University of Houston. Currently, he's teaching English at Cascadia Community College and coordinating 826 Seattle's adult writing workshop series: "How to Write Like I Do." He's also the father of two boys who provide plenty of poetic moments, some of which he finds time to write about.

Jason Whitmarsh earned his B.A. in mathematics from the University of Chicago and an M.F.A. in poetry from the University of Washington. His poems have appeared in many literary journals, including *Yale Review, Harvard Review, Ploughshares,* and *Fence*. His book, *Tomorrow's Living Room*, won the 2009 May Swenson Poetry Award. He lives in Seattle with his wife and children.

Jay Thompson writes poetry, essays, and Dungeons & Dragons fiction, and he keeps a column on poetry at the blog for *The Kenyon Review.* He has had poems and essays featured in *EOAGH*, *Pleiades Caffeine Destiny, Rain Taxi Online, The Laurel Review,* and *Microfilme*.

Jeannine Hall Gailey is the current Poet Laureate of Redmond, Washington, and has authored two books of poetry: *Becoming the Villainess* (Steel Toe Books, 2006) and *She Returns to the Floating World* (Kitsune Books, 2011). She teaches a graduate seminar course at National University in California and was on the core faculty of the Centrum Young Artists Project in Port Townsend, Washington. Gailey's work addresses feminist issues of power in mythology and comic book cultures, turning fairy tale stepmothers into empathetic characters, and holding up a mirror to contemporary American culture's images of powerful women. *She Returns to the Floating World* deals with feminine transformations in the personae of characters from Japanese folk tales, anime, and manga.

Jeremy Halinen is the author of *What Other Choice*, winner of the Exquisite Disarray First Book Poetry Contest. He is a co-editor and co-founder of *Knockout Literary Magazine*. He holds an MFA in Creative Writing from Eastern Washington University.

Many people know him as Johnny Horton, but for the past year he has been using **John Wesley Horton** as a pen name to avoid Google confusion with 1950s rockabilly singer Johnny Horton (and because it sounds so much like the Bob Dylan record *John Wesley Harding*). John co-directs the University of Washington's summer creative writing program in Rome, Italy. One decade ago, John set foot in Rome for the first time and it felt like a homecoming. Four years later, his father, who had (in John's words) "been adopted by one of the WASPiest families in Chicago, Illinois," admitted his biological mother was Italian.

Judith Roche was born and raised in Detroit in an active union-organizing family and retains deep ties to Michigan and to the Midwest, though she has lived in Seattle for many years. Her most recent poetry collection, *Wisdom of the Body* (Black Heron Press, 2007), won an American Book Award and was nominated for a Pushcart. She is a mother, a grandmother and a sister.

Julie Larios teaches on the faculty of the Vermont College of Fine Arts in their Writing for Children MFA program. She has published four books of poetry for children: *On the Stairs, Have You Ever Done That?* (both Front Street), *Yellow Elephant* (named a Boston Globe-Horn Book Honor Book), and *Imaginary Menagerie* (both Harcourt). She is the winner of a Pushcart Prize, has been twice included in the annual *Best American Poetry* series for her adult poetry, and was granted a fellowship by the Washington State Arts Commission/Artist Trust. She was also the librettist for a pocket opera (music by Dag Gabrielson) performed by members of the New York City Opera for their 2011 Vox Series.

Karen Finneyfrock is a poet, novelist, and teaching artist in Seattle. Her second book of poems, *Ceremony for the Choking Ghost* (Write Bloody Press), was released in 2010, and her young adult novel, *The Sweet Revenge of Celia Door,* is due out from Viking Children's Books in 2013. She is a former writer-in-residence at Richard Hugo House in Seattle and teaches for Seattle Arts and Lectures' Writers in the Schools program. In 2010, Karen traveled to Nepal as a Cultural Envoy through the United States Department of State to perform and teach poetry; in 2011, she did a reading tour in Germany sponsored by the US Embassy.

Kary Wayson's poems have appeared or are forthcoming in *Poetry Northwest, The Alaska Quarterly Review, The Nation,* FIELD, and *The Best American Poetry*. Her chapbook, *Dog & Me*, was published in 2004 by LitRag Press. Kary teaches Poetry at Richard Hugo House.

Kate Lebo's poems have appeared in *Best New Poets 2011*, *AGNI*, *Poetry Northwest*, and *Bateau*, among others. She's an editor for *Filter*, recipient of a Nelson Bentley Fellowship, a 4Culture grant, and a Soapstone Writing Residency. Kate's zine, *A Commonplace Book of Pie*, is a collection of facts both real and imagined about everyone's favorite dessert. An award-winning pie maker, Kate hosts a semi-regular, semi-secret pie social called Pie Stand. The week after she graduated from the University of Washington's MFA program she started a pie school, called Pie School.

Kathleen Flenniken's first book, *Famous* (University of Nebraska, 2006), won the Prairie Schooner Book Prize in Poetry and was named a Notable Book by the American Library Association. Her poems have appeared in *The Iowa Review, Prairie Schooner, Poetry, The Writer's Almanac, Poetry Daily, American Life in Poetry*, and many others. Her second collection, *Plume*, has been selected by Linda Bierds for the Pacific Northwest Poetry Series and will be published in Spring 2012 by University of Washington Press.

Kelli Russell Agodon is the author of *Letters from the Emily Dickinson Room* (White Pine Press, 2010), winner of the ForeWord's Book of the Year Award in Poetry. She is also the author of *Small Knots* and the chapbook, *Geography*. Her work has appeared in magazines and journals such as *The Atlantic, Prairie Schooner*, and *North American Review* as well as on *The Writer's Almanac* with Garrison Keillor. Kelli is the editor of Seattle's literary journal, *Crab Creek Review*, and the co-founder of Two Sylvias Press. She lives in the Pacific Northwest where she is a mountain biker and kayaker, and is currently at work on her third book of poems.

Kevin Craft's first book, *Solar Prominence* (2005), was selected by Vern Rutsala for the Gorsline Prize from Cloudbank Books. His poems, reviews, and essays have appeared widely in such places as *Poetry, AGNI, Verse, The Alaska Quarterly Review, The Stranger*, and *Poetry Northwest*. Craft has received fellowships from the MacDowell Colony, the Bogliasco Foundation (Italy), the Carmargo Foundation (France), and the Washington State Arts Commission/Artist Trust. He also teaches Creative Writing for the University of Washington's Summer in Rome Program, and is editor of *Mare Nostrum*.

Martha Silano began writing poetry in elementary school but did not get up the courage to attend her first formal poetry workshop until she was twenty-five. She went on to receive her MFA in Creative Writing from the University of Washington.

Megan Snyder-Camp grew up in Baltimore and received an MFA in Poetry from the University of Washington. She has worked as a New York City Parks Inspector, a secretary for a surgical robotics lab, with Teach for America in Los Angeles, as an EMT, a Quaker meetinghouse caretaker, and a freelance writer. Her first collection, *The Forest of Sure Things*, won the 2008 Tupelo Press/Crazyhorse First Book Award.

Meghan McClure studies at the Rainier Writing Workshop, the MFA program at Pacific Lutheran University, and is co-director of Zimbags, a non-profit organization. She helps edit *A River & Sound Review* and her work has been published in *Mid-American Review, roger: an art & literary journal, Superstition Review, Bluestem*, and *Floating Bridge Review*. Meghan lives in Auburn, Washington, with her husband and animals.

Michael Spence served four years as a naval officer aboard the USS John F. Kennedy after graduating with a degree in creative writing from the University of Washington in 1974. Spence lives in Tukwila, Washington, and has spent the last twenty-five years as a public-transit bus driver in the Seattle area. He has contributed poems to more than a dozen journals and an anthology of northwestern poets. Spence's collections include *The Spine, Adam Chooses*, and *Crush Depth.*

Molly Tenenbaum is the author of three poetry collections: *The Cupboard Artist* (Floating Bridge Press, 2012), *Now* (Bear Star Press, 2007), and *By a Thread* (Van West & Co, 2000). Honors include a Hedgebrook residency and a 2009 Washington State Artist Trust Fellowship. She's also a musician, playing Appalachian string band music; her CDs are *Instead of a Pony* and *Goose & Gander.* She lives in Seattle.

Oliver de la Paz is the author of three collections of poetry, *Names Above Houses, Furious Lullaby* (Southern Illinois U. Press, 2001, 2007), and *Requiem for the Orchard* (U. of Akron Press, 2010), which was selected winner of the Akron Prize for Poetry. He is the co-editor of *A Face to Meet the Faces: An Anthology of Contemporary Persona Poetry* (U. of Akron Press, 2012). He co-chairs the advisory board of Kundiman, a nonprofit organization dedicated to the promotion of Asian American Poetry and serves on the Association of Writers and Writing Programs Board.

Peter Pereira is a physician, a poet, and the founder of Floating Bridge Press. His work has appeared in numerous publications, including *Poetry, Virginia Quarterly Review,* and several anthologies, including *Best American Poetry.* He has received the "Discovery"/The Nation Award and

Hayden Carruth Poetry Prize. In his chapbook, *The Lost Twin* (2000), and two full-length collections, *Saying the World* (2003) and *What's Written on the Body* (2007), he seamlessly traverses his favorite themes, which include his work as a primary care provider at an urban clinic in Seattle, domestic life, suffering and the human condition, and the slippage of language.

Pimone Triplett is the author of *The Price of Light* (Four Way Books, 2005) and *Ruining the Picture* (Triquarterly/Northwestern, 1998). She holds an MFA from the University of Iowa. She is also a teacher, having taught at various universities and workshops, including the University of Washington and the Warren Wilson MFA Program for Writers.

Rebecca Hoogs' poems have appeared in *Poetry*, *AGNI*, and *Crazyhorse*, among others. She has also written a chapbook called *Grenade*. Rebecca has received fellowships from the MacDowell Colony and Artist Trust of Washington State. She acts as the Director of Education Programs and curates and hosts the Poetry Series for Seattle Arts & Lectures.

Richard Kenney has published three books of poetry: *The Evolution of the Flightless Bird*, *Orrery*, *The Invention of the Zero*, and *The One-Strand River*. He has received fellowships from the Guggenheim and MacArthur foundations, as well as the Rome Prize in Literature and a Lannan Literary Award. He teaches at the University of Washington in Seattle.

Richard Wakefield's collection *East of Early Winters* was published by the University of Evansville Press in 2006 and won the Richard Wilbur Award. His sonnet "Petrarch" won the 2010 Howard Nemerov Award. In May 2012, Able Muse Press published his second collection of poetry, *A Vertical Mile*. For over twenty-five years, Richard has been a critic of fiction and poetry for the *Seattle Times*.

Rick Barot was born in the Philippines and grew up in the Bay Area, but currently resides in Tacoma, Washington. He attended Wesleyan University, the Iowa Writers' Workshop, and was a Stegner Fellow and Jones Lecturer in Poetry at Stanford University. Rick has received a fellowship from the National Endowment for the Arts and has taught at numerous universities. Rick's first collection of poetry, *The Darker Fall*, received the Kathryn A. Morton Prize in Poetry—his second collection, *Want*, won the 2009 Grub Street Book Prize. His poems and essays have appeared in the *New Republic*, *Poetry*, *Kenyon Review*, *Virginia Quarterly Review*, and other publications.

Poet **Sarah Galvin** writes for *The Stranger*'s music and nightlife blog, *Line Out*. You can find out more about Sarah and her writing on her blogs *The Pedestretarian* and *Tea Party.*

Sierra Nelson has been writing, teaching, and performing in Seattle for more than fourteen years. She published her lyrical choose-your-own-adventure book *I Take Back the Sponge Cake* (Rose Metal Press) in spring 2012, and her poems have appeared in journals such as *Poetry Northwest, Crazyhorse,* and *Tin House*, among others. Nelson earned her MFA in Poetry from the University of Washington and is a MacDowell Colony fellow and 2011 Hackney National Literary Award winner for poetry. Nelson is also co-founder of the innovative literary performance art groups The Typing Explosion and the Vis-à-Vis Society.

Susan Parr was born in Las Cruces, New Mexico, and grew up in Florida, Central Illinois, West Virginia, and Ohio. She was educated at Barnard College, and studied at Leningrad State University during the summer of 1988. In 2005 Susan left her job as a self-taught graphic designer and earned an MFA in Creative Writing from the University of Washington. In 2009, her first collection of poems, *Pacific Shooter* (Pleiades Press), won the Lena-Miles Wever Todd Poetry Prize. Concurrently, she began to gradually lose her sense of hearing.

Susan Rich currently lives in Seattle and teaches at Highline Community College where she runs the reading series Highline Listens: Writers Read Their Work. She has authored three complete collections of poetry: *The Cartographer's Tongue / Poems of the World, Cures Include Travel,* and *The Alchemist's Kitchen*—her individual poems have been widely published. Susan has received awards from PEN USA, The Times Literary Supplement, and Peace Corps Writers, as well as a variety of fellowships including an Artists Trust Fellowship from Washington State and a Fulbright Fellowship in South Africa.

PORTLAND

Andrew Michael Roberts is the author of *something has to happen next*, which was awarded the Iowa Poetry Prize. He has two chapbooks: *Dear Wild Abandon* and *Give Up*, and is the recipient of a national chapbook fellowship from the Poetry Society of America and a distinguished teaching award from the University of Massachusetts Amherst. A cyclist and runner, he lives in Portland with his wife Sarah, and is currently a nursing student at Oregon Health and Science University.

Camille Rankine is the author of *Slow Dance with Trip Wire*, selected by Cornelius Eady for the Poetry Society of America's 2010 New York Chapbook Fellowship. She was also the recipient of a 2010 "Discovery"/ Boston Review Poetry Prize. Her poetry has been published in several magazines and journals, including *American Poet, Boston Review,* and *O, The Oprah Magazine.* She is Assistant Director of the Graduate Program in Creative Writing at Manhattanville College.

Carl Adamshick is the author of the poetry collection *Curses and Wishes*, which won the Stafford/Hall Award for Poetry at the 2012 Oregon Book Awards. He is also the recipient of an Oregon Literary Fellowship from Literary Arts and the 2010 winner of the Walt Whitman Award and the William Stafford poet-in-residence at Lewis & Clark College. His work has been published in *Harvard Review, American Poetry Review,* and *Narrative,* among others. Carl currently lives in Portland, where he co-founded and runs Tavern Books.

Carlos Reyes is a prolific poet and well-known translator. He has published four collections of his own poetry including his most recent title, *Pomegranate, Sister of the Heart* (2012), as well as numerous translations. His honors include the receipt of a Heinrich Boll Fellowship, the Ethel Fortner Award from St. Andrews College, and a poet-in-residence position at Joshua Tree National Park. He currently lives in Portland, where he is the publisher and editor of Trask House Books, Inc.

Cecelia Hagen is the author of *Entering* (Airlie Press, 2011) and two chapbooks, *Fringe Living* (26 Books Press) and *Among Others* (Traprock Books). Her poetry, reviews, and nonfiction have been published by *Rolling Stone, Prairie Schooner, Poet & Critic,* and many other publications. Her work also is, or will be included, in public art projects at the Kaiser Medical Center in Hillsboro, Oregon, Lane Community College, and downtown Eugene.

Clemens Starck is the author of five poetry books: *Journeyman's Wages, Studying Russian on Company Time, China Basin, Traveling Incognito,* and *Rembrandt, Chainsaw.* He has received the Oregon Book Award as well as the William Stafford Memorial Poetry Award from the Pacific Northwest Booksellers Association. He lives in the country outside of Dallas, Oregon, in the Willamette Valley.

Crystal Williams is the author of three collections of poems, most recently *Troubled Tongues*, winner of the 2009 Naomi Long Madgett Poetry Award. She has just completed a fourth collection of poems, titled *Detroit as Barn.* Widely anthologized, her poems also appear in journals and publications such as *The American Poetry Review, The Northwest Review,* and *Ms.* magazine, among others. Crystal holds an MFA from Cornell University, and has received fellowships and grants from The MacDowell Arts Colony, Literary Arts, the Oregon Arts Commission, and Money for Women/Barbara Deming Memorial Fund. She is dean of institutional diversity and associate professor of creative writing at Reed College.

Dan Raphael is a poet, performer, editor, reading arranger, and author of more than thirteen poetry collections. He has also collaborated with jazz saxophonist Rich Halley and drummer Carson Halley to create a performance CD. Dan has performed more than 250 times, in places like Wordstock, Bumbershoot, Powell's Books, Eastern Oregon University, Portland Jazz Festival, and other Portland venues. He edited *NRG Magazine* for seventeen years, and has hosted Poetland in the past.

Daneen Bergland's poems have appeared in various journals and magazines, including *Propeller, The Denver Quarterly,* and *Poet Lore.* Daneen has received a fellowship from Oregon Literary Arts, a Pushcart Prize nomination, and awards from the Academy of American Poets.

David Biespiel is the president of the Attic Institute, a haven for writers in Portland. He is the author of four books of poetry, including *The Book of Men and Women, Wild Civility, Pilgrims & Beggars,* and *Shattering Air,* as well as a book on creativity, *Every Writer Has a Thousand Faces.*

Dean Gorman lives in Portland, where he plays in the bands The Tumblers and Sweet William's Ghost. He graduated from the Vermont College MFA program and co-founded Pilot Books and Magazine. His work has appeared in *Gulf Coast, The Indiana Review,* and *Forklift Ohio,* among others.

Donna Henderson's poems have appeared widely in magazines and anthologies, and earned her two Pushcart Prize nominations. *The Eddy Fence* is her first full-length poetry collection. She is a founding member of the poetry and classical piano performance trio Tonepoem, based at Western Oregon University, and also a founding member of Airlie Press. Donna maintains a psychotherapy practice in Monmouth, Oregon, and teaches creative writing at Willamette University.

Emily Kendal Frey is the author of the full-length poetry collection *The Grief Performance* (Cleveland State University Poetry Center, 2011), which was selected for the Cleveland State Poetry Center's 2010 First Book Prize. She also won the Poetry Society of America's 2012 Norma Farber First Book Award. Emily's poetry also appears in other publications including *Octopus* and *The Oregonian*, and she's the author of numerous chapbooks. Emily received an MFA from Emerson College, and currently lives in Portland.

Floyd Skloot's seventeen books include the poetry collections *The Snow's Music* (LSU Press, 2008) and *Selected Poems: 1970–2005* (Tupelo Press, 2008), winner of a Pacific Northwest Book Award. He has won three Pushcart Prizes, and his work has been included twice each in *The Best American Essays, Best American Science Writing, Best Spiritual Writing*, and *Best Food Writing* anthologies.

Henry Hughes is the author of three poetry collections: *Men Holding Eggs* (winner of the 2004 Oregon Book Award), *Moist Meridian* (2011), and *Shutter Lines* (2012). He is the editor of the anthology, *The Art of Angling: Poems About Fishing*, and his commentary on new poetry appears regularly in *Harvard Review*.

Jennifer Richter's book *Threshold* has been a national bestseller, and her work has appeared in *Poetry, Poetry Northwest*, and *The Missouri Review*, among others. She was awarded a Wallace Stegner Fellowship and Jones Lectureship in Poetry by Stanford University, where she taught in the Creative Writing Program for four years. Jennifer teaches for Stanford's Online Writer's Studio and as Visiting Poet in Oregon State University's MFA Program; she lives in Corvallis, Oregon, with her children and her husband, novelist Keith Scribner.

Jerry Harp is the author of three books of poetry: *Creature* (Salt Publishing, 2003), *Gatherings* (Ashland Poetry Press, 2004), and *Urban Flowers, Concrete Plains* (Salt Publishing, 2006). He co-edited *A Poetry*

Criticism Reader with Jan Wiessmiler. His essays and reviews appear regularly in *Pleiades*. He teaches at Lewis & Clark College.

Jesse Lichtenstein is a journalist, poet, screenwriter, and teacher. He is a founder and co-director of the Loggernaut Reading Series and currently spends most of his time in Oregon.

Though now pursuing a PhD in Creative Writing at the University of Denver, **Jesse Morse** will always consider the Northwest one of his three homes. He's had various pieces published in various places (like *Bombay Gin* and *Fiction Brigade*), and Portland-based C_L Press put out a chapbook called *Rotations*, with a lot more Eric Chavez poems of a completely different nature. Jesse spends much of his time playing outdoors with his labradane, Hank.

John Morrison's book, *Heaven of the Moment*, won the Rhea & Seymour Gorsline Poetry Competition. He received his MFA from the University of Alabama. John's poetry has appeared in numerous national journals including the *Cimarron Review, Poet Lore,* and *Poetry East*, among others. John has taught poetry at the University of Alabama, Washington State University, and in the Literary Arts Writers in the Schools program where he served as director from 2006–2009. He is currently an Adjunct Fellow at the Attic Institute.

John Sibley Williams is the author of six chapbooks and winner of the HEART Poetry Award. He has served as an acquisitions manager at Ooligan Press, been an agent and publicist, and holds an MFA in Creative Writing and MA in Book Publishing. A few previous publishing credits include: *Inkwell, Bryant Literary Review, Cream City Review, The Chaffin Journal, The Evansville Review, RHINO, Rosebud, Ellipsis, Flint Hills Review*, and various other fiction and poetry anthologies.

Judith Barrington is the author of three poetry collections, most recently *Horses and the Human Soul,* selected by Oregon's State Library for "150 Books for the Sesquicentennial." She has also recently published two poetry chapbooks, including the Robin Becker Award-winning, *Lost Lands.* Her *Lifesaving: A Memoir* was winner of the Lambda Literary Award. Her other awards include The Dulwich International Poetry Prize and The Stuart Holbrook Award from Literary Arts. She teaches literary memoir in the University of Alaska's MFA program and lives in Oregon.

Kaia Sand is the author of the book *Remember to Wave* (Tinfish Press, 2010)—also the name of a walk Sand leads in North Portland. Both the book and walking tour investigate political history and current goings-on. She is also the author of the poetry collection *interval* (Edge Books, 2004), and co-author with Jules Boykoff of *Landscapes of Dissent* (Palm Press, 2008). She participates in the Dusie Kollektiv, recently creating a broadside of her embroidered 8 ft. drop cloth poem. She is a member of PEN American Center and teaches at Pacific University.

Kathleen Halme grew up in Wakefield, a post-mining and logging town in Michigan's upper peninsula, but now lives in Portland. She completed her MFA in Creative Writing at the University of Michigan, where her work was awarded the Hopwood Creative Writing Award. Her honors include a National Endowment for the Arts fellowship in poetry, a National Endowment for the Humanities fellowship in anthropology, and an Oregon Literary Fellowship. Her poems have appeared widely in journals, including *Poetry, Ploughshares*, and *Virginia Quarterly Review*, among others. Her three books of poetry are: *Every Substance Clothed* (winner of the University of Georgia Press Contemporary Poetry Series and the Balcones Poetry Prize), *Equipoise*, and *Drift and Pulse*.

Kirsten Rian is a widely published essayist and poet, with work appearing in magazines, international literary journals, and anthologies. She is the author of three books, including the forthcoming *Chord*, to be released in early 2013 through Wordcraft. She co-authored the now-sold-out Northwest anthology, *Walking Bridges Using Poetry as a Compass* (Urban Adventure Press). Her anthology of Sierra Leonean poetry, *Kalashnikov in the Sun* (Pika Press), was released in 2010; this collection is in every classroom in Sierra Leone, and is used as a textbook on discussing and processing war at the Kroc Institute for International Peace Studies Institute of the University of Notre Dame.

Leah Stenson earned an MA in English Literature in 1971, and went on to do editorial work for the Soka Gakkai, serve as Managing Director of the Oregon Peace Institute for three years, actively support various nonprofit organizations, and publish multiple chapbooks. Leah has co-authored an English textbook as well as articles and book reviews, some of which have appeared in *The Oregonian*, *The World Tribune*, and *School Library Journal.* Her poetry has appeared in *Oregon Literary Review, Northwest Women's Journal*, and *Verseweavers*, among others.

Lex Runciman teaches at Linfield Collge, where the English department offers degrees in literature and in creative writing. This shows how the culture has changed: when Lex was an undergraduate (at a good school in California), the curriculum offered a single course in creative writing—which he took as a freshman. When, at the end of the term, Lex said to the teacher, "That was fun, I want to do more of it," the response he heard was "you can't—we have one course called Imaginative Writing, and you've just finished it."

Lisa Steinman, Kenan Professor of English & Humanities at Reed College, is the author of three books about poetry including *Invitation to Poetry* (Blackwell), four volumes of poetry, and a poetry chapbook. Winner of the Oregon Book Award for *All That Comes to Light*, Lisa's work has also received recognition from the National Endowment for the Arts, the National Endowment for the Humanities, and the Rockeller Foundation, among others. Her poems have appeared in such journals as *Notre Dame Review, Chariton Review, Chicago Review*, and *Michigan Quarterly,* among others. She also co-edits the poetry magazine *Hubbub.*

Lucas Bernhardt is a freelance writer and editor who also teaches writing at Portland State University. He earned MA degrees in English Literature and in Writing from PSU, and an MFA from the Iowa Writers' Workshop. He is the managing editor of *Propeller* magazine, and his own work has appeared in a number of magazines.

Mary Szybist grew up in Pennsylvania, and earned her MFA from the Iowa Writers' Workshop, where she was also a Teaching-Writing Fellow. Mary's poetry has appeared in *Denver Quarterly, The Iowa Review,* and *Poetry,* among others. She received a fellowship from the National Endowment for the Arts, and is one of two recipients of the 2009 Witter Bynner Award. Her collection of poems, *Granted* (Alice James Books, 2003) won the 2003 Beatrice Hawley Award from Alice James Books and the 2004 Great Lakes Colleges Association New Writers Award. Mary is currently an assistant professor of English at Lewis & Clark College.

About becoming a poet, **Maxine Scates** says, "I'm not sure that I really had a choice; poetry was the form that called to me as a way of making sense of the world, and at eighteen or nineteen it was the only thing anyone had ever told me I was good at—though now I suspect good meant promising! In its way, 'The Giants' was a given poem—once I'd found the metaphor, the poem flowed easily (which is not always the case) but I recall particular pleasure in writing this poem."

Paul Merchant is a poet, translator, and the William Stafford Archivist at Lewis & Clark College. He taught for many years at Warwick University before moving to Oregon. His recent translations from modern Greek include *Monochords* by Yannis Ritsos, published in 2007 by Trask House Press, and *Twelve Poems about Cavafy*, published by Tavern Books in 2010.

Oregon's sixth Poet Laureate, **Paulann Petersen**, has published five full-length books of poetry, most recently *The Voluptuary* (Lost Horse Press). Her poems have appeared in many journals and anthologies, including *Poetry*, *The New Republic*, and *Prairie Schooner*, among others. A former Stegner Fellow at Stanford University and the recipient of the 2006 Holbrook Award from Oregon Literary Arts, she serves on the board of Friends of William Stafford, organizing the January Stafford Birthday Events.

Penelope Scambly Schott is the author of five chapbooks and eight full-length books of poetry. Her verse biography, *A is for Anne: Mistress Hutchinson Disturbs the Commonwealth*, received the 2008 Oregon Book Award for Poetry. Her most recent book, *Crow Mercies* (2010), was awarded the Sarah Lantz Memorial Poetry Prize from Calyx Press. Penelope lives in Portland and teaches an annual poetry workshop in Dufur, Oregon.

Peter Sears graduated from Yale University and the Iowa Writers' Workshop. He won the 1999 Peregrine Smith Poetry Competition and the 2000 Western States Poetry Prize for his book, *The Brink*. He has published several full length collections and his work can also be found in a variety of magazines and literary journals, as well as on the radio series, *The Writer's Almanac*. His most recent full-length book is titled *Green Diver*. Sears founded and manages the Oregon Literary Coalition and co-founded the nonprofit organization Friends of William Stafford.

Robert Duncan Gray—who authored the introduction to the *Alive at the Center* anthology—is an Englishman who grew up in the Black Forest of southwestern Germany. He studied art at the University of California, Santa Barbara, and currently lives and works in Portland. He is an editor and webmaster for *HOUSEFIRE* and the author of *CABBAGE LANGUAGE* (forthcoming on HOUSEFIRE, 2012) and *cloud / moustache* (NAP, 2012). Rob works on writing, reading, performing, photography, painting, drawing, and music.

Rodney Koeneke is the author of the poetry collections *Musee Mechanique* (BlazeVOX, 2006) and *Rouge State* (Pavement Saw, 2002), and numerous chapbooks. His writing has appeared in *Aufgabe, The Nation,* and ZYZZYVA, among others. Since moving to Portland in 2006, he's written a poetry-focused blog, *Modern Americans* and reviewed nearly 300 books of (mostly contemporary) poetry on Goodreads. An essay on the poet Hannah Weiner can be found online at the University of Buffalo's Electronic Poetry Center.

Sarah Bartlett lives in Portland, and reads poetry for *Tin House.* She received a MFA from Emerson College. Her chapbook *A Mule-Shaped Cloud* (Horse Less Press), co-authored with Chris Tonelli, came out in 2008. Her work has appeared in a number of literary journals including *Diagram, Past Simple, Bat,* and *Rhino,* among others.

Scot Siegel's most recent book of poetry is *Thousands Flee California Wildflowers* (Salmon Poetry, 2012), and his most recent work appears in *American Poetry Journal, High Desert Journal,* and *Open Spaces: Voices of the Northwest* (University of Washington Press, 2011). Siegel lives near Portland, where he works as a town-planning consultant and serves on the board of the Friends of William Stafford. He edits *Untitled Country Review,* an online journal of poetry and visual art.

Sid Miller, the founding editor of the poetry journal *Burnside Review* and a Pushcart Prize nominee, has seen wide publication of his work. He has three full-length poetry collections to his name, his chapbook *Quietly Waiting* was published in 2004 by White Heron Press, and his work has also appeared in other publications including *The Oregonian, Portland Review,* and *High Desert Journal.* He lives in Portland.

Susan Denning is a writer who lives in Portland. She edited the online magazine *Caffeine Destiny* for thirteen years.

W. Vandoren Wheeler's poems have appeared in *Swink, H_ngM_n, and Bat City Review,* among others. He earned an MFA from Warren Wilson, and edited Marylhurst University's *M Review* for two years. He teaches composition, creative writing, and literature at Portland Community College. His manuscript, *The Accidentalist,* won the 2012 Dorothy Brunsman Prize.

Willa Schneberg is the author of three poetry collections: *Box Poems; In The Margins of the World* (winner of the Oregon Book Award for Poetry);

and *Storytelling in Cambodia.* Among the publications and anthologies in which her poems have appeared are: *American Poetry Review; The Year's Best Fantasy and Horror* (St. Martin's Press); and *I Go the Ruined Place: Contemporary Poems in Defense of Global Human Rights* (Lost Horse Press). In fall of 2012, her interdisciplinary exhibit entitled "The Books of Esther" was on view at the Oregon Jewish Museum.

All poems are published with permission of the poet, in addition to the permission of any previous publisher, as cited below.

VANCOUVER

"After the Tsunami," Robin Susanto. Reprinted with permission from *Quills Canadian Poetry*

"a lightness dances," Diane Tucker. Reprinted with permission from *Bright Scarves of Hours*. Kingsville, ON: Palimpsest Press, 1997.

"Appleton," Heather Haley. Reprinted with permission from *Three Blocks West of Wonderland*. Victoria, BC: Ekstasis Editions, 2009.

"Attempts to Know the Past," Aislinn Hunter. Reprinted with permission from *The Possible Past*. Richmond, BC: Raincoast Books, 2005.

"Beer, Blood, & Bukowski," Shannon Rayne. Reprinted from *Poetry is Dead, Issue* 3. poetryisdead.ca

"Border Boogie (1969)," Susan McCaslin. Reprinted with permission from Allan Briesmaster, ed., *Crossing Lines: Poets who Came to Canada in the Vietnam Era*, Toronto: Seraphim Editions, 2008, and *Demeter Goes Skydiving*, Edmonton, AB: University of Alberta Press, 2011.

"Cabin Fever," Anna Swanson. Reprinted with permisson from *the Night's Also*. Toronto: Tightrope Books, 2010.

"Cell Phone," Christopher Levenson. Reprinted with permission from *Local Time*. Ottawa, ON: Stone Flower Press, 2006.

"Crows," Sandy Shreve. Reprinted with permission from *Suddenly So Much*. Holstein, ON: Exile Editions, 2005.

"Desdamona (Durga)," Joanne Arnott. First appeared in *The New Chief Tongue*, chieftongue.blogspot.com/

"Everyday things," Lilija Valis. Reprinted with permission from *Freedom on the Fault Line*. Parker, CO: Outskirts Press, 2012.

"The Goodnight Skirt," Raoul Fernandes. Originally published as "In the Treehouse." Reprinted from *Emerge 2009*.

"Hollow," David Zieroth. Reprinted with permission from *The Fly in Autumn*, Harbour Publishing, 2009, www.harbourpublishing.com.

"Manning Park in the Dark," Evelyn Lau. Reprinted with permission from *Living Under Plastic*. Fernie, BC: Oolichan, 2010.

"mount pleasant," Nikki Reimer. Reprinted with permission from *[sic]*. Calgary, AB: Frontenac House, 2010.

"Nadine," Russell Thornton. Reprinted with permission from *The Human Shore*, Harbour Publishing, 2006, www.harbourpublishing.com.

"the next growing season: a glossary," Renée Sarojini Saklikar. Reprinted with permission from *thecanadaproject.com*.

"Offering," Rita Wong, *forage*, Nightwood Editions, 2007, www.nightwoodeditions.com

"Our Salt Spring Island Dinner," Chris Gilpin. Originally printed in *Contemporary Verse 2*, www.contemporaryverse2.ca/

"Rushing Undergrowth," Kate Braid. Reprinted with permission from *To This Cedar Fountain*. Halfmoon Bay, BC: Caitlin Press, 2012.

"Stealing Anatomies," Kraljii Elee Gardiner. Reprinted with permission from *The Writers Caravan Anthology* Vancouver, BC: Otter Press, 2011.

"The Stone," Ibrahim Honjo. Reprinted with permission from *Roots in the Stone*. Markham, ON: Books, Inc., 1990.

"Tongue," Susan Cormier. Reprinted with permission from *All Wound Up*. Vancouver, BC: Ripple Effect Press, 2002.

"The Wailing Machine," Rob Taylor. Reprinted with permission from *The Other Side of Ourselves*. Markham, ON: Cormorant Books, 2011.

"The Weight of Dew," Daniela Elza. Reprinted with permission from *The Weight of Dew*. Salt Spring Island, BC: Mother Tongue Publishing, 2012.

"What we heard about the Canadians," Rachel Rose. Originally appeared in *Rattle*, #35, Summer 2011, www.rattle.com/poetry/print/30s/i35/

SEATTLE

"Ablation as the Creation of Adam," Oliver de la Paz. Reprinted with permission from *Requiem for the Orchard.* Akron, OH: University of Akron Press, 2010.

"Anniversary," Jason Whitmarsh. Reprinted with permission from *Tomorrow's Living Room*. Logan, UT: Utah State University Press, 2009.

"Auguries," Richard Kenney. Reprinted from *Southwest Review* and *Best American Poetry 2007*. New York: Scribner, 2007.

"Bloomery," Molly Tenenbaum. Reprinted with permission from *Now*. Cohasset, CA: Bear Star Press, 2007.

"Boondocks," Heather McHugh. From *Upgraded to Serious*. Copyright © 2009 by Heather McHugh. Reprinted with the permission of The Permissions Company, Inc. on behalf of Copper Canyon Press, www.coppercanyonpress.org.

"Commute," Rebecca Hoogs. Reprinted from *Notre Dame Review*.

"Estrangement in Athens," Brian Culhane. From *The King's Question*. Copyright © 2008 by Brian Culhane. Reprinted with the permission of The Permissions Company, Inc. on behalf of Graywolf Press, Minneapolis, Minnesota, www.graywolfpress.org.

"From the Tower," Heather McHugh. From *Upgraded to Serious*. Copyright © 2009 by Heather McHugh. Reprinted with the permission of The Permissions Company, Inc. on behalf of Copper Canyon Press, www.coppercanyonpress.org.

"Hidden," Christine Deavel. Reprinted with permission from *Woodnote*. Cohasset, CA: Bear Star Press, 2011.

"History of Paranoia," Jason Whitmarsh. Reprinted with permission from *Tomorrow's Living Room*. Logan, UT: Utah State University Press, 2009.

"History of Translation" Jason Whitmarsh. Reprinted with permission from *Tomorrow's Living Room*. Logan, UT: Utah State University Press, 2009.

"Hometown (A Savior Saves by Not Saving)," Christine Deavel. Reprinted with permission from *Woodnote*. Cohasset, CA: Bear Star Press, 2011.

"Honeymoon," Rebecca Hoogs. Reprinted from *Notre Dame Review*.

"Humans" Elizabeth Austen. Reprinted from *Crab Creek Review*.

"King Limbo," Belle Randall. Reprinted from *The Coast Starlight*, WordTech Communications, August 26, 2010.

"Kinship," Frances McCue. Reprinted with permission from *The Bled*. Hadley, MA: Factory hollow press, 2010.

"Man in the Street," Heather McHugh.

From *Upgraded to Serious*. Copyright © 2009 by Heather McHugh. Reprinted with the permission of The Permissions Company, Inc. on behalf of Copper Canyon Press, www.coppercanyonpress.org.

"Monster," Karen Finneyfrock. Reprinted with permission from *What to Read in the Rain*. Seattle, WA: 826 Seattle, 2012.

"My New Life," Molly Tenenbaum. Reprinted with permission from *Old Voile*. Tucson, AZ: New Michigan Press, 2004.

"Not Towards a Real, Towards Another," Sierra Nelson. Reprinted with permission from *Crazyhorse* 78 (Fall 2010).

"Nursemaid's Elbow," Peter Pereira. Reprinted with permission from *Best American Poetry 2007*. New York: Scribner, 2007.

"Plato's Bad horse," Deborah Woodard. Reprinted with permission from *Plato's Bad Horse*. Cohasset, CA: Bear Star Press, 2006.

"Processional," Emily Warn. From *The Shadow Architect*. Copyright © 2008 by Emily Warn. Reprinted with permission of The Permissions Company, Inc. on behalf of Copper Canyon Press, www.coppercanyonpress.org.

"Receding Universe Rag," Susan Parr. Reprinted with permission from *Pacific Shooter*. Baton Rouge, LA: LSU Press, 2009.

"Robot Scientist's Daughter," Jeannine Hall Gailey. Reprinted with permission from *The Portland Review*.

"Saudade," Michael Spence. Reprinted with permission from *Crush Depth*. Kirksville, MO: Truman State University Press, 2009.

"Sea Creatures of the Deep," Megan Snyder-Camp. Reprinted with permission from *The Forest of Sure Things*. North Adams, MA: Tupelo Press, 2010.

"Seward Park" J. W. Marshall. Reprinted with permission. First published in *Field Magazine* 81 (Fall 2009).

"So Long Moon Snail," Christianne Balk. Reprinted with permission from *Barrow Street Journal* (Spring 1999).

"West Coast," Ed Skoog. From *Mister Skylight*. Copyright © 2009 by Ed Skoog. Reprinted with permission of The Permissions Company, Inc. on behalf of Copper Canyon Press, www.coppercanyonpress.org.

"What I will tell the aliens," Martha Silano. Reprinted with permission from *The Little Office of the Immaculate Conception*. Ardmore, PA: Satumalia, 2011.

"What the Sea Takes," Holly J. Hughes. Reprinted with permission from *Boxing the Compass*. Seattle: Floating Bridge Press, 2007.

PORTLAND

"Accidents of Trees," Daneen Bergland. Reprinted with permission from *Hayden's Ferry Review*, Issue 41 (Fall/ Winter 2007-08).

"A Man Who Was Afraid of Language," Jerry Harp Reprinted. with permission from *Notre Dame Review: The First Ten Years*, University of Notre Dame Press, 2009, and Creature, Cambridge, UK: Salt Publishing, 2003. First published in *Notre Dame Review* 6 (Summer 1998).

"Annunciation: Eve to Ave," Mary Szybist. From *Incarnadine*. Copyright © 2012 by Mary Szybist. Reprinted with the permission of The Permissions Company, Inc. on behalf of Graywolf Press, Minneapolis, Minnesota, www.graywolfpress.org. First appeared in *The Iowa Review*.

"Appetite," Paulann Petersen. Reprinted with permission from *The Wild Awake*, Confluence Press, 2002, and *Poetry* 178, no. 4 (July 2001).

"Avulsion" Kathleen Halme. From *Equipoise*. Copyright © 1998 by Kathleen Halme. Reprinted with permission of The Permissions Company, Inc. on behalf of Sarabande Books, Inc. www.sarabandebooks.org

"Bloodline," Paulann Petersen. Reprinted with permission from *The Voluptuary*. Sandpoint, ID: Lost Horse Press, 2010.

"Dismantling," Clemens Starck. Reprinted with permission from *Journeyman's Wages. Ashland, OR:* Story Line Press, 1995.

"Distant Friends," Lisa Steinman. Reprinted with permission from *Carslaw's Sequences*. University of Tampa Press, 2003.

"Don't Ask, Don't Tell," Scot Siegel. Reprinted with permission from *Thousands Flee California Wildflowers.* Cliffs of Moher, County Clare, Ireland: Salmon Poetry, 2012.

"Drawing Lesson," Cecelia Hagen. Reprinted with permission from *Caffeine Destiny*, www.caffeinedestiny.com.

"Enlightenment," Crystal Williams. Forthcoming in *Angles of Ascent: A Norton Anthology of Contemporary African American Poetry.* New York: W.W. Norton, 2013. Reprinted with permission from *Connotation Press: An Online Artifact* (April 2010).

"First Ice," Donna Henderson. Reprinted with permission from *The Eddy Fence*, Monmouth, OR: Airlie Press, 2009, and *A Fine Madness* 9 (2004).

"Heaven Described," Mary Szybist. Copyright © 2012 by Mary Szybist. Reprinted with the permission of The Permissions Company, Inc. on behalf of the author. First appeared in *Mare Nostrum*.

"I am pregnant with my mother's death," Penelope Scambly Schott. Reprinted with permission from *Six Lips*. Woodstock, NY: Mayapple Press, 2009.

"Icelandic Church," John Sibley Williams. Reprinted with permission from *From Colder Climates*. Rocklin, CA: Folded Word, 2012.

"In My Alternate Life," Lex Runciman. Reprinted with permission from *Starting from Anywhere*. County Clare, Ireland: Salmon Poetry, 2009.

"In the Montparnasse Cemetery," Carlos Reyes. Reprinted with permission from *Pomegranate, Sister of the Heart*. Sandpoint, IL. Lost Horse Press, 2012.

"Invitation," Mary Szybist. From *Incarnadine*. Copyright © 2012 by Mary Szybist. Reprinted with the permission of The Permissions Company, Inc. on behalf of Graywolf Press, Minneapolis, Minnesota, www.graywolfpress.org. First appeared in *Electronic Poetry Review*.

"Kansas, 1973," Floyd Skloot. Reprinted with permission from *Selected Poems: 1970–2005*. North Adams, MA: Tupelo Press, 2008.

"Late Nap," Peter Sears. Reprinted with permission from *Luge*. Corvallis, OR: Cloudbank, 2009

"Night Landing," Kirsten Rian. Reprinted with permission from *Broad River Review* (2011).

"Night Train," Leah Stenson. Reprinted with permission from *Heavenly Body*. Georgetown, KY: Finishing Line Press, 2011.

"Paper Mill," Henry Hughes. Reprinted with permission from *basalt* 6, no. 1 (Spring 2011).

"Souls Under Water," Judith Barrington. Reprinted with permission from *Postcard from the Bottom of the Sea*. Portland, OR: The Eighth Mountain Press, 2008.

"Tantalus," Paul Merchant. Reprinted with permission from *Stones*. Exeter, UK: Rougemont Press, 1973.

"That Time Again," Dan Raphael. Reprinted with permission from *Windfall: A Journal of Poetry of Place* (Spring 2007) and *The State I'm In*. Nine Muses, 2007.

"The Bells of St. Bavo Sing Scat," Willa Schneberg. Reprinted with permission from *Storytelling in Cambodia*. Corvallis, OR: Calyx Books, 2006.

"The Giants," Maxine Scates. Reprinted with permission from *Undone*. Kalamazoo, MI: Western Michigan University (New Issues Poetry & Prose), 2011.

"There was a war, the end," Andrew Michael Roberts. Reprinted with permission from *New Ohio Review* 3 (Spring 2008).

"Threshold:," Jennifer Richter. Reprinted with permission from *Threshold*. Southern Illinois University Press, 2010.

"Without," Cecelia Hagen. Reprinted with permission from *Caffeine Destiny*, www.caffeinedestiny.com (website discontinued December 2012).

ACKNOWLEDGEMENTS

OOLIGAN PRESS

Ooligan Press takes its name from a Native American word for the common smelt or candlefish. Ooligan is a general trade press rooted in the rich literary life of Portland and the Department of English at Portland State University. Ooligan is staffed by students pursuing master's degrees in an apprenticeship program under the guidance of a core faculty of publishing professionals.

Acquisitions
Tony Anderson
J. Adam Collins
John Sibley Williams

Permissions
Katie Allen
Heather Frazier
Tara Lehmann
Jonathan Stark
Kristen Svenson

Editors
Katie Allen
Kylie Byrd
Gino Cerruti
Heather Frazier
Rachel Hanson
Rebekah Hunt
Tiah Lindner
Amber May
Isaac Mayo
Anne Paulsen
Ashley Rogers
Jonathan Stark
Kristen Svenson
Jennifer Tibbett
Amreen Ukani
Amanda Winterroth

Cover Design
J. Adam Collins

Interior Design
Poppy Milliken
Lorna Nakell

Miscellaneous Design
Brandon Freels
Mandi Russell
Kelsey Yocum

Online materials
Kate Burkett

E-book Design
Kai Belladone
Anna Smith

Logo Design
Tristen Jackman
Lisa Shaffer

Marketing & Sales
Emily Gravlin
Kristin Howe
Kathryn Ostendorff

Project Management
J. Adam Collins
Joel Eisenhower
Amber May
Tina Morgan
Kathryn Ostendorff
Rachel Pass
Jessica Snavlin
Jonathan Stark
John Sibley Williams

OOLIGAN
PRESS

369 Neuberger Hall
724 SW Harrison Street
PO Box 751
Portland, Oregon 97207
Phone: 503.725.9748 | Fax: 503.725.3561
ooligan@ooliganpress.pdx.edu | ooligan.pdx.edu

Ooligan Press is a general trade publisher rooted in the rich literary tradition of the Pacific Northwest. A region widely recognized for its unique and innovative sensibilities, this small corner of America is one of the most diverse in the United States, comprising urban centers, small towns, and wilderness areas. Its residents range from ranchers, loggers, and small business owners to scientists, inventors, and corporate executives. From this wealth of culture, Ooligan Press aspires to discover works that reflect the values and attitudes that inspire so many to call the Northwest their home.

Founded in 2001, Ooligan is a teaching press dedicated to the art and craft of publishing. Affiliated with Portland State University, the press is staffed by students pursuing master's degrees in an apprenticeship program under the guidance of a core faculty of publishing professionals.

Ordering information:

Individual Sales: All Ooligan Press titles are available through your local bookstore, and we encourage supporting independent booksellers. Please contact your local bookstore, or purchase online through Powell's, Indiebound, or Amazon.

Retail Sales: Ooligan books are distributed to the trade through Ingram Publisher Services. Booksellers and businesses that wish to stock Ooligan titles may order directly from IPS at (866) 400-5351 or customerservice@ingrampublisherservices.com.

Educational and Library Sales: We sell directly to educators and libraries that do not have an established relationship with IPS. For pricing, or to place an order, please contact us at operations@ooliganpress.pdx.edu.

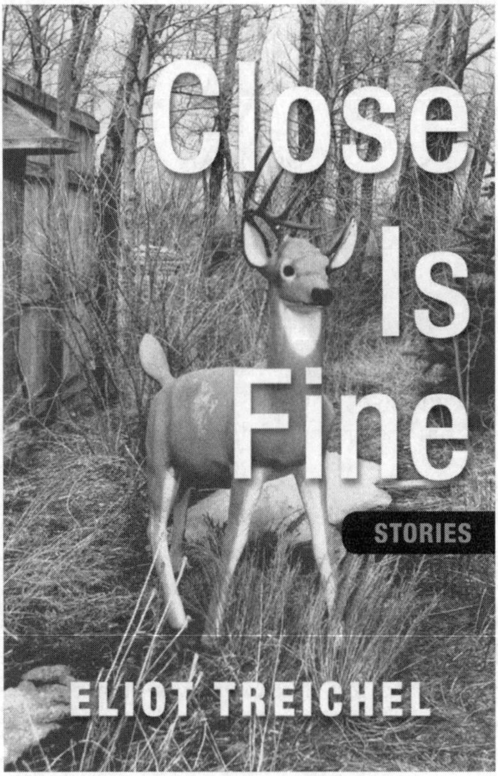

Close Is Fine

a short story collection
Eliot Treichel

fiction | $14.95 | 168 pages
5½" x 8½" | softcover | ISBN13: 978-1-932010-45-9

OOLIGAN
PRESS

Like a Polaroid snapshot, this finely wrought collection of short stories gives us a brief glimpse into the quirky and complex lives of rural town inhabitants. As the characters struggle to define their individuality and reconcile their ideals with ordinary life, we are witness to their unique self-discoveries. At times mournful and haunting, this story collection celebrates the nobility of simple life, of striving and failing without ever losing hope.

Ooligan Press • Portland, Oregon • ooligan.pdx.edu

American Scream: Palindrome Apocalypse

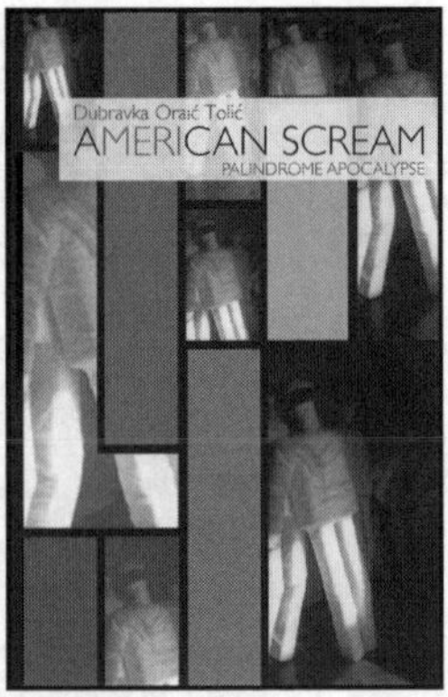

by Dubravka Oraić Tolić

poetry | $14.95
240 pages | 6" x 9" | softcover
ISBN13: 978-1-93-2010-10-7

Utopia—we all want our own, but who pays for it and at what price? Croatian poet Dubravka Oraić Tolić delivers a masterful, thought-provoking answer with exquisite language and imagery in the epic poem *American Scream*. Complementing *American Scream* is *Palindrome Apocalypse*—a palindrome that is artful in both technique and story—presented side-by-side with the Croatian original to preserve its visual effect. Together, Oraić Tolić's poems explore dark themes of social and individual selfishness in pursuit of dreams and the unintended consequences of those efforts; examine the tension between a nation's dream of freedom and the outworking of that dream; capture the heart of pre- and post-war Croatia, yet speak universally of the pain of bringing one's visions to life.

Dot-to-Dot, Oregon

by Sid Miller

poetry | $13.95
88 pages | 6" x 9" | softcover
ISBN13: 978-1-93-2010-29-9

Sid Miller explores seven routes from the coast to the mountains, from inner-city Portland to the Idaho border. *Dot-to-Dot, Oregon*, a collection of fifty poems, travels through the cities, towns, and monuments of Oregon. Using these locales as a background, three voices narrate the author's loving but critical relationship with the state he calls home.

"Connect the dots? If you do you'll discover some strange and wonderful constellations superimposed over familiar topography… *Dot-to-Dot* is a lyrical and, at times, a dark and hilarious guide to the blue lines (secondary roads) of the Beaver State. So before you head out to Shoetree (Don't look for it on a highway map.), Nyssa (a damsel in metaphysical distress?), or some other exotic location in the Beaver State, take a look at Sid Miller's new book or, better yet, take it with you on your rambles."

— Carlos Reyes

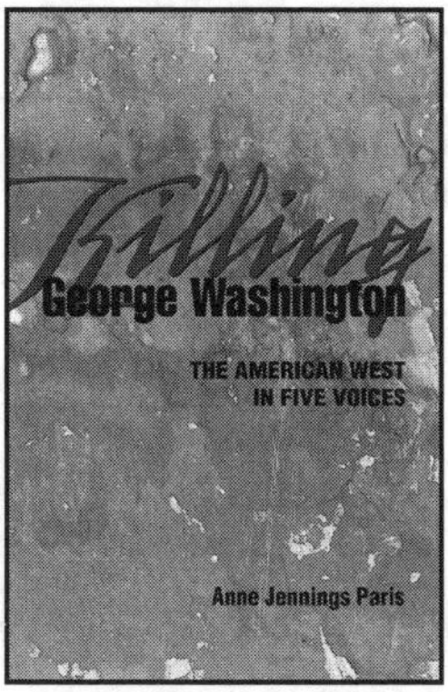

Killing George Washington: The American West in Five Voices

by Anne Jennings Paris

poetry | $13.95
120 pages | 6" x 9" | softcover
ISBN13: 978-1-93-2010-30-5

Killing George Washington tells the story of the American frontier as it moves west. Anne Jennings Paris, in a collection of narrative poems, imagines the voices of the forgotten historical figures of Lewis Wetzel, a notorious Indian killer; York, the slave who accompanied Lewis and Clark; Charity Lamb, Oregon's first convicted murderess; Ing Hay, a Chinese immigrant who made a name for himself as a doctor; and Mary Colter, an architect who helped shaped the western landscape. Exploring the American consciousness, these poems question our shared heritage through the personal stories of legends.

Oregon Stories

Edited by Ooligan Press

poetry | $16.95
272 pages | 6" x 9" | softcover
ISBN13: 978-1-932010-33-6

This collection of 150 personal narratives from everyday Oregonians explores the thoughts, feelings, and experiences of the people who live in this unique state. *Oregon Stories* shows why people cherish this state and why Oregonians strive to keep Oregon unique and beautiful while celebrating its rich history and diverse opportunities. Drawn from the Oregon 150 Commission's Oregon Stories website project—in which a variety of citizens submitted personal stories that will resonate with any Oregon resident—this book collects the stories and histories of the people that make this place home. The subject of these stories varies widely—some authors tell detailed family histories, while others describe exciting travels throughout Oregon's beautiful landscape. This book features local contributors who reside in different communities all over the state, resulting in a publication truly representative of Oregonians as a whole. Read much more about the Oregon Stories project as part of the Oregon 150 Official Sesquicentennial Commemoration on the main website.

You Have Time for This:

Contemporary American Short-Short Stories

Edited by Mark Budman & Tom Hazuka

fiction | $11.95
135 pages | 5" x 7½" | softcover
ISBN13: 978-1932010-17-6

Love, death, fantasy, and foreign lands, told with brevity and style by the best writers in the short-short fiction genre. *You Have Time for This* satiates your craving for fine literature without making a dent in your schedule. This collection takes the modern reader on fifty-three literary rides, each one only five hundred words or less. Mark Budman and Tom Hazuka, two of the top names in the genre, have compiled an anthology of mini-worlds are as diverse as the authors who created them. Contributing writers include Steve Almond, author of *My Life in Heavy Metal* and *Candyfreak*; Aimee Bender, author of *The Girl in the Flammable Skirt*; Robert Boswell, author of five novels, including *Century's Son*; Alex Irvine, author of *A Scattering of Jades*; L. E. Leone, who writes a weekly humorous column about food and life for the *San Francisco Bay Guardian*; Justine Musk, author of dark-fantasy novels, including *Blood Angel*; Susan O'Neill, writer of nonfiction and fiction with a book of short stories called *Don't Mean Nothing; Short Stories of Vietnam*; and Katharine Weber, author of several novels, including *Triangle*. From Buddha to beer, sex to headless angels, there's a story here for everyone. In *You Have Time for This* you will find: flash fiction from forty-four authors, works from across the globe, highly regarded authors from all types of genres, fresh work from emerging writers, and fifty-three stand alone pieces that tie the world together.

Enjoy. You have time for this.

"A really good flash fiction is like a story overheard at a bar—personal, funny, dangerous, and sometimes hard to believe. *You Have Time for This* distills those qualities and many others into quick tall tales by writers who are as talented as they are magical."

—Kevin Sampsell, author of *Beautiful Blemish* and publisher of Future Tense Publishing

Ooligan Press • Portland, Oregon • ooligan.pdx.edu